CineTech

CineTech

Film, Convergence and New Media

Stephen Keane

First published 2007 by
PALGRAVE MACMILLAN
Houndmills, Basingstoke, Hampshire RG21 6XS and
175 Fifth Avenue, New York, N.Y. 10010
Companies and representatives throughout the world

PALGRAVE MACMILLAN is the global academic imprint of the Palgrave Macmillan division of St. Martin's Press, LLC and of Palgrave Macmillan Ltd. Macmillan® is a registered trademark in the United States, United Kingdom and other countries. Palgrave is a registered trademark in the European Union and other countries.

ISBN-13: 978–1–4039–3693–6 hardback
ISBN 10: 1–4039–3693–5   hardback
ISBN-13: 978–1–4039–3694–3 paperback
ISBN-10: 1–4039–3694–3   paperback

This book is printed on paper suitable for recycling and made from fully managed and sustained forest sources.

A catalogue record for this book is available from the British Library.

A catalog record for this book is available from the Library of Congress.

10   9   8   7   6   5   4   3   2   1
16   15   14   13   12   11   10   09   08   07

Printed in China

For Rachel

Contents

Introduction

CineTech will explore the key issues and activities resulting from the convergence between film and new media technologies. We will begin by looking at the ways in which film and cinema have themselves undergone major changes in recent years. The transition from **analogue** to **digital** processes has come to transform film at the levels of production and postproduction, and is beginning to have similar effects on cinema distribution and exhibition. We will then move on to the ways in which film has entered into convergence with new media forms and technologies. From amateur to independent filmmaking, digital video and user-friendly software packages have enabled a broader base for the creation of films. Principally, however, the current situation has been regarded in terms of consumption. This has obvious commercial implications but within a broader context that is much more complex than identifying dominant sources and unwitting audiences and consumers. A look at this new network of access and availability across a wide range of media forms shows that there has been an increase in the information surrounding films, a proliferation of outlets for the viewing of film, and associated products that bring various modes of engagement and activity into the equation. We are no longer invited simply to view films. We are now being invited to participate.

This is an interdisciplinary study that will be of value to both Film and New Media students. It will take a particularly 'high-tech' approach to the study of film and a 'comparative' approach to new media. It will examine the ways in which (a) Film Studies has dealt with issues surrounding technology and (b) how key aspects of New Media Studies can be applied through to film. To state that this is an interdisciplinary study is not merely the result of combining Film with New Media Studies. It is also the very practical result of looking at the increasing **convergence** of film and new media in recent years. Born out of the same drive that made 'media fusion', 'multimedia' and 'synergy' such popular business terms in the 1990s,

1

convergence is a means of extending the commercial range of any particular film or entertainment product through its connection with other outlets, the ultimate goal being that of the same branded content played out across multiple media. Beyond this dominant commercial remit, however, I am much more interested in the *principles*, *processes* and *effects* of convergence. I will be looking at these in terms of, first, contradiction and, then, synthesis.

Convergence can be said to represent either a dissipation of the particular qualities of film and cinema or a challenging reconfiguration of filmmaking, film viewing and the business of film. On one level, this study seeks to highlight the distinct properties of film and cinema, and examine the new technologies ostensibly responsible for maintaining film viewing and cinema going as special events. But it is with the realization that there is a lot more to the current context than simply watching films on the big screen. Films can, of course, be viewed from the comfort of the home but recent developments such as home cinema, the internet and videogames also mean that the home supplies all of the entertainment that people require. The potential contradictions are those between 'cinema going' and 'home entertainment', 'viewing' and 'interactivity'. These can also, however, be broached in terms of synthesis. Which is to say that, far from losing its distinct properties, film can be said to have joined in with this new matrix of media forms.

Throughout this study, therefore, we will progress from the 'internal' to the 'external', from recent technological developments within film and cinema through to the diversity of convergence with new media forms and technologies. This will be done by following the overall circuit of film from industry to audiences.

The main questions that I will be addressing are as follows:

- What are the distinct technological properties of film and cinema?
- How have those qualities been altered or enhanced in recent years through the adoption of new digital processes?
- What are the distinct and convergent properties of new media?
- What happens when film and cinema enter into convergence with new media?

In Chapter 1, I will introduce the main screen forms to be covered throughout this study – cinema, television, computers and videogames. Chapters 2 and 3 are the most directly film-based chapters and will examine the ways in which digital processes have entered into major aspects of film production and postproduction. One of the key features of this book is its use of case studies. Here, I will be taking a form-and-content approach to the different areas of study, establishing the main arguments relating to the forms and practices under discussion in each chapter and applying them to close analysis of relevant texts. In Chapters 2 and 3, I will be looking at relevant independent films and Hollywood blockbusters. Reference to specific film franchises like the *Star Wars* saga and *Matrix* trilogy will be made throughout this study. As well as providing for continuity of reference, such film series exist as the most apparent examples of contemporary high-tech filmmaking practices and allied commercial strategies. In Chapters 4 and 5, I will move on to the two principal new media forms to be examined in this study – the internet and videogames. These chapters deal with notions of information and interactivity: first, the ways in which the internet has been used by studios and film fans, and then the main comparisons and contrasts that can be made between films and videogames. The case studies in these two chapters will focus in on relevant websites and videogames. Chapter 6 will take the form of a complete case study exploring the convergent campaign surrounding the two *Matrix* sequels, *Reloaded* and *Revolutions*. Here, I will be exploring the films' advances in special effects and the use of recent promotional forms such as DVDs and videogames. I will end this study by looking at the very latest developments in the convergence of film, cinema and new media in terms of digital cinema and home viewing, issues surrounding film content available on the internet, mobile gaming, and micro-media.

Overall, *CineTech* will provide students with a topical study of film, convergence and new media, using up-to-date examples of relevant texts and developments. My aim is to get *inside* the main media forms, to look at the distinct properties of film, television, the internet, videogames and micro-media, and the ways in which these forms have also entered into convergence with each other in recent years. The book also provides source notes on relevant DVDs, websites and videogames, and a glossary in order to further your understanding of key terms and concepts.

Having provided a brief introduction to the scope and structure of this study, the following represents a much more detailed explanation of the main issues to be explored within each of the chapters.

Chapter 1 Screens

[keywords: screens, technology, film, cinema, new media]

In this chapter I will be using the figure of the screen in order to make initial comparisons and contrasts between cinema, television, computers and videogames. While there is a marked difference between cinema and computers, 'spectators' and 'users', the histories of each of the respective forms also point to the fact that they have never been wholly separate. There are long-standing links between cinema and television, for example, and videogames can be played on computers and television screens. This puts the recent business of convergence – of providing for a smooth flow of content across all media forms – into further context. The purpose of this chapter, therefore, is exactly that of *initial* comparisons and contrasts. Framing the book as a whole with regard to 'big screen versus small', we will return to the very latest developments in the concluding chapter, key distinctions still remaining but with the different screens having merged much more in terms of viewing and activity.

Film will assume a number of guises throughout this study – as 'software' run through different forms of hardware, and as 'content' played out across numerous platforms from promotional websites to DVDs. First of all, however, there is an essential distinction to be made between *film* and *cinema*. As Stephen Heath argues, the difference between film and cinema is what we see 'in frame' and 'on screen'. A key distinction within **apparatus theory** of the 1970s and 1980s, cinema is regarded as the overall institution of film; not merely the primary site for film viewing but also the main intersection between industry and ideology. In Heath's complex deconstruction, the film '*text* . . . is a particular product of that industry' and cinema the '*machine* . . . seized exactly between industry and product as the stock of constraints and definitions from which film can be distinguished as *specific signifying practice*' (Heath 1976: 7).

Historical accounts of film look at developments in technique: in cinematography, editing, special effects, and so on. Although there is significant overlap, historical accounts of cinema have looked at developments in technology – the structural elements that have gone towards maintaining the overall, situational film experience understood in terms of audiences experiencing films on the big screen (see, for example, Cook and Bernink 1999; Monaco 2000; Cook 2004).

The three main developments in this respect are sound, colour and widescreen. In the first section of Chapter 1, I will principally be looking at developments in widescreen from CinemaScope to IMAX. This will allow us to establish some of the key industrial factors underpinning the development of cinema as well as outlining the basic conditions of spectatorship.

Like cinema, television is an 'old medium' that has undergone a constant process of renewal. The first step to another screen form, television is the medium that has shared most with cinema, from initial competition in the 1950s through to providing films with an enduring afterlife beyond the silver screen. While the basic send-and-receive mechanisms of television have remained the same, modes of transmission have advanced through cable, satellite and digital television, and numerous 'appliances' have been introduced such as the VCR and DVD players. This has led to more choice in film viewing but there are still fundamental differences between watching films at the cinema and viewing them at home. In the second section of Chapter 1, therefore, I will be looking at the long-standing interplay between cinema and television, and what happens when the cinema spectator becomes the film viewer.

The final two sections of Chapter 1 will bring us on to computers, the internet and videogames. Where film and television are essentially old media brought into line with the new, computers and videogames almost automatically qualify as new media. The tendency to look back on the 1970s and 1980s as the time when cinema more fully entered into the home, piped through cable or slotted into VCRs, parallels the miniaturization and domestication of technology as a whole during that time. The 1980s, in particular, were the decade when the remote control, satellite television, personal computers, videogame consoles, CD players and the Sony Walkman became a fluid fixture of people's daily lives. This smaller, more pervasive and intimate technological turn of the 1980s is very much the starting point for **Cyberculture Studies**. Cyberculture Studies can be regarded as the speculative forerunner of New Media Studies. While Cyberculture Studies looked at the ways in which we were becoming more and more like posthuman cyborgs, New Media Studies begins with the practical recognition that now is the time of digital media. Beginning in the late 1990s, to a certain extent New Media Studies has yet to achieve a stable identity. This is not merely because of its relatively novel status but also because of its innately interdisciplinary nature. As David Silver argues, whichever term we care to use – 'internet/cyberculture/digital culture/new media/fill-in-the-blank studies' – this is still a 'meta-field' of study (Silver 2004: 55). As a starting point, however, New Media Studies interrogates notions of the 'new', looking at the ways in which 'old' media have developed in accordance with new technologies and the ways in which new media have come to enter into our lives in recent years. As Roger Silverstone states in response to the question, 'What's new about new media?', the new can be defined in terms of 'continuity', 'change' and 'novelty' (Silverstone 1999: 10–12). Where continuity and change keep new media in context, novelty ensures that new media never settles and is always reaching for the next big thing.

A provisional list of new media would be helpful at this point, to be followed by more up-to-date examples in the outline to my Conclusion. Two of the most important introductions to the study of new media, particularly in the ways in which they look at continuity as well as change, are Jay David Bolter and Richard Grusin's *Remediation: Understanding New Media* (1999) and Lev Manovich's *The Language of New Media* (2001). The most common examples of new media from both studies are:

computer animation; digital art; digital photography; digital video; film and cinema; the internet; multimedia; television; videogames; virtual reality.

To state that computers and videogames almost automatically qualify as new media is to highlight the fact that while we can trace their origins back to calculating machines of the nineteenth century or the first computer games of the 1960s, they have only recently become recognizable media forms. The main developments in this respect include: videogame consoles first entering the home in the 1970s; the introduction of the personal computer in the early 1980s; videogaming becoming big business in the 1980s and 1990s; the advent of the World Wide Web in the early 1990s; and the internet boom of the late 1990s. What are the main formal differences and similarities between cinema and computers; and what happens when we are invited to participate in increasingly cinematic videogames? Reduced in terms of size and scope, film is nevertheless expanded in terms of information and activity.

Chapter 2 Digital film and Chapter 3 Digital special effects

[keywords: analogue, digital, digital video, high-definition, special effects]

Chapters 2 and 3 are the most directly film-based chapters in this book and explore the ways in which digital processes have come to transform key aspects of film production and postproduction. Digital film and special effects provide us with examples of internal convergence. Which is to say that, with the adoption of computer-generated imaging (CGI) in the late 1980s and digital video (DV) in the late 1990s, filmmaking has been able to pioneer as much as it has simply appropriated digital practices. Those critics foretelling 'the death of cinema' in light of its becoming thoroughly digital are more accurately holding on to the familiar, ingrained properties of the analogue (see Usai 2001; Dixon 2003). There are those, however, who argue the transition from analogue to digital more in terms of continuity, adaptation and evolution (see Harley 1999; Rosen 2001; Nowell-Smith and Thomas 2003).

In Chapter 2, I will be introducing digital processes in relation to film production. I will begin by examining the claim that the digital image is more 'dynamic' and 'flexible' than the analogue image. I will then look at the ways in which digital practices have entered other aspects of filmmaking such as editing and sound. In the second half of this chapter I will focus on the use of digital video by independent filmmakers and the repercussions of high-definition (HD) processes on independent and mainstream filmmaking. I will end this chapter with the first two case studies to be explored in this book – the experimental *Timecode* (2000) and the DV horror films, *My Little Eye* (2002) and *28 Days Later* (2002).

In Chapter 3, I will move on to special effects and the realm of the blockbuster. The point at which aspects of film technique most directly meet up with notions of cinematic spectacle, the study of computer-based special effects has proven the first and foremost approach to new technologies of the screen (see, for example, Landon 1992; Sobchack 1993; Baker 1993; Bukatman 1993). As Michael Allen argues in his analysis of technological developments from widescreen to CGI: 'The drive behind much of the technical development in cinema since 1950 has been geared towards both a greater or heightened sense of "realism" and a bigger, more breath-taking realisation of spectacle' (Allen 1998: 127). Analyses of digi-tal special effects have been particularly drawn to this ongoing sleight of hand regarding spectacle and realism, 'persuading audi-ences that the simulated and the artificial are the real and the actual, that they *can* believe their eyes' (Allen 1998: 128). Studies of digi-tal special effects have also tended to address the ways in which images essentially created in *computers* transfer to the largely *photographic* medium of film (see Caughie and Cubitt 1999; Allen 2002; Pierson 2002). In Chapter 3, therefore, I will be looking at digital special effects in terms of contradiction and synthesis; that is, the ways in which they have successfully or otherwise been inte-grated into the existing palette and parameters of film. Looking at this in terms of film form, aesthetics and narrative, I will be look-ing at a range of genres from science fiction to animated feature films. In my chosen case studies I will be looking at the 'spectacle versus narrative' debate as applied to *Star Wars Episode II: Attack of the Clones* (2002) and the use of digital actors as related to the character of Gollum in *The Lord of the Rings: The Two Towers* (2002).

Chapter 4 Films, fans and the internet and Chapter 5 Films and videogames

[keywords: the internet, audiences, fandom, videogames, play]

Chapters 4 and 5 will bring us on to the two main new media forms to be studied in this book – the internet and videogames. I have already established the ways in which new media are first defined in comparison and contrast with existing media This is particularly important when dealing with film. But the comparative approach of New Media Studies also helps to distinguish the particular qualities of new media. The internet isn't simply a magazine, for example, and videogames aren't simply toys. New Media Studies has progressed through an identifiable canon of studies (see, in particular, Bolter and Grusin 1999; Lunenfeld 1999; Manovich 2001; Harries 2002a; Everett and Caldwell 2003; Lister *et al.* 2003; Thorburn and Jenkins 2003). In all of these, the comparative approach is also *developmen-tal*. While comparisons and contrasts with existing media provide for initial definitions, therefore, the next step lies in understanding the ways in which existing media have been transformed by new media technologies and that, ultimately, new media require new ways of thinking. How might this comparative and developmental approach be used to distinguish the internet and videogames?

As Jay David Bolter and Richard Grusin argue, new media work through 'immediacy' and 'hypermediacy'. Promising more instant and authentic experiences, every successive medium always starts, paradoxically, by drawing attention to itself. With particular regard to the internet, for example, it might well be that a computer user is looking for familiar content such as art, magazine features, news or film trailers. It's possible to access that content immediately but the particular hypermediate property of PCs and the internet is that the user is able to access all of that information at once:

> In digital technology, as often in the earlier history of Western represen-
> tation, hypermediacy expresses itself as multiplicity. If the logic of
> immediacy leads one either to erase or to render automatic the act of
> representation, the logic of hypermediacy acknowledges multiple acts of
> representation and makes them visible. Where immediacy suggests a
> unified visual space, contemporary hypermediacy offers a heterogeneous
> space, in which representation is conceived of not as a window on to the
> world, but rather as 'windowed' itself – with windows that open on to
> other representations or other media. (Bolter and Grusin 1999: 33–4)

Bolter and Grusin go on to outline four levels of remediation. As in the example above, first of all, new media simply make use of old or existing sources. This is the 'straightforward' access to content available in prior media form. In the next level, improvements become apparent in the ways that the original material is accessed or organized. Where Bolter and Grusin's third level of remediation is particular to alternative and avant-garde practices within digital video and video art, the final level is much more complete in terms of the overall form and content of the original medium being repli-cated and enhanced by new media:

> Finally, the new medium can remediate by trying to absorb the older
> medium entirely, so that the discontinuities between the two are mini-
> mized. The very act of remediation, however, ensures that the older
> medium cannot be entirely effaced; the new medium remains dependent
> on the older one in acknowledged or unacknowledged ways (Bolter and
> Grusin 1999: 47)

Here, the comparisons become very refined, whether videogames that make use of cinematic elements, films that make use of digital aesthetics, or the ways in which the internet remediates aspects of television. What all of these examples ultimately point to is that convergence is a two-way process in which the new benefits from existing modes of information and representation, and the old is updated in such a way as to secure further relevance. Looked at in this way, new media are much more evolutionary than revolutionary.

In *The Language of New Media*, Lev Manovich follows the same levels of remediation to a large extent but with a particular eye on computerization and visual culture:

> The computerization of culture not only leads to the emergence of new cultural forms such as computer games and virtual worlds; it redefines existing ones such as photography and cinema. I therefore also investigate the effects of the computer revolution on visual culture at large. How does this shift to computer-based media redefine the nature of static and moving images? What is the effect of computerization on the visual languages used by our culture? What new aesthetic possibilities become available to us? (Manovich 2001: 9)

Manovich's main argument is that computerization wouldn't have taken hold in the ways that it has if it hadn't become cultural. This is what distinguishes computer science and computer culture, the abstract language and inner-workings of computers applied through to a diversity and familiarity of uses. A comparable term to 'computerization' is Manovich's use of 'cinematographic', referring to the ways in which key aspects of computer culture have come to communicate through the basic principles of cinema. In particular, there is the use of the 'mobile camera' from the simple navigation of word-processing documents to first- and third-person perspectives in videogames. As Manovich states: '*the visual culture of a computer age is cinematographic in its appearance, digital on the level of its material, and computational (i.e. software driven) in its logic*' (Manovich 2001: 180). If this speaks to a certain familiarity, however, there are also the ways in which new media work through the essentials of computerization. As Manovich argues, two defining characteristics of computer culture are 'the database' and 'navigable space'. Allowing us access to information on the one hand, and allowing for psychological immersion and engagement on the other, Manovich uses webpages and search engines as key examples of the former and videogames as examples of the latter. Although not always separate from each other, Manovich regards the database and navigable space as effectively distinguishing the internet and videogames from the library, museum, or literary and cinematic narratives (Manovich 2001: 214–17).

In Chapter 4, I will be exploring the circulation of film-related information on the internet from 'official' film sites to 'unofficial' fan sites. In the first part I will examine the ways in which official sites promote films and often work in creating or catering for fans of certain films and genres. Then I will progress to closer consideration of online fandom, the ways in which film fans are dependent on central sources of information but also go on to create their own alternative communities. My case studies will focus on two key fan sites in order to monitor fans' expectations of *Star Wars Episode III: Revenge of the Sith* (2005) and responses to *Sin City* (2005).

In Chapter 5, I will be examining the main comparisons and contrasts between films and videogames. While adaptations provide for the most obvious comparisons between the two, the interplay between films and videogames has also been regarded in terms of shared business practices, the ways in which blockbuster films have come to be likened to videogames, and the ways in which videogames make use of cinematic elements. Rather than simply presenting us with comparable cinematic narratives, however, videogames also work through the principles of play, navigation and interactivity. The case studies in this chapter will focus on the *Resident Evil* games and films, and a videogame that makes extensive use of cinematic elements, *Metal Gear Solid 2: Sons of Liberty* (2001).

Chapter 6 Entering the matrix and Conclusion

[keywords: promotion, merchandising, digital cinema, home entertainment, micro-media]

Chapter 6 will take the form of a complete case study focusing on the convergent campaign surrounding the 2003 release of *The Matrix Reloaded* and *The Matrix Revolutions*. Looking at the films themselves in terms of narrative, meaning and special effects, I will then progress to consideration of the accompanying websites, DVDs, animated shorts and videogames. As Simone Murray suggests, we are currently undergoing a 'third wave' of media convergence.

Following on from the rise of multinational conglomerates and the use of common digital operating systems, the third wave is that of 'content streaming', which 'represents media conglomerates' attempt to recreate economies of scale for high-cost releases by aggregating revenue streams from multiple ancillary markets'. In this current wave, films become the 'anchor product' subsequently 'repurposed' through numerous outlets from pay-per-view television and DVDs to theme park attractions and videogames (Murray 2003: 10). The potential objection to paying for similar content several times is directed through brand loyalty. From *Harry Potter* to *Bridget Jones's Diary*, markets are built around specific demographics, the main aim of which is 'to encourage in consumers an emotional investment in the market brand' (Murray 2003: 13–14). This brand loyalty ultimately translates into content loyalty. The most distinct feature of the campaign for the two *Matrix* sequels was that it made particularly organized and extensive use of narrative cross-referencing across numerous promotional outlets. Leading on from the films themselves, I will then move on to the overall campaign for the sequels and end with *The Animatrix* and the *Enter the Matrix* videogame. Through the use of new media, the situation has now shifted from promotion to participation. Like the characters in the films, perhaps, we have all entered the matrix.

In the Conclusion to this study I will look at the very latest developments in film, convergence and new media. Returning to big screen developments on the one hand and small screen developments on the other, I will adopt the same structure as Chapter 1 but less in terms of 'new media' as 'current media'. Having provided a provisional list of new media earlier in this introduction, the main developments that I will be looking at are:

- digital cinema
- digital television
- home cinema
- alternative formats to DVD
- film content available on the internet
- issues surrounding digital piracy
- convergence between television and the internet
- mobile gaming
- online gaming
- micro-media

Promising ease of distribution and further enhancement of the big screen experience, digital cinema will ultimately lead to 'projection' being replaced by 'transmission'. Completing the overall digital takeover of cinema from production to exhibition, films are also available through more outlets than ever before, from the internet to current micro-media. Convergence is bringing computers and television together, and the most recent videogame consoles are also complete entertainment systems. Regarded in these terms, the future of cinema might not be so much a matter of getting people out of the house as distinguishing film from all other parts of the flow.

1 Screens

The figure of the screen is at once the most containing and convergent of forms. Although the cinema screen, television screen and computer screen can still be said to retain their principal structures, convergence has lead to the transfer and merging of actual content. This has an enormous effect on the previous separation between 'viewing' and 'activity'. Writing in 2000, for example, Anne Friedberg states:

> As this millennium draws to an end, cinema – a popular form of entertainment for almost a century – has been dramatically transformed. It has become embedded in – or perhaps lost in – the new technologies that surround it. One thing is clear . . . the differences between the media of movies, television, and computers are rapidly diminishing. This is true both for technologies of production . . . and for technologies of reception and display . . . The movie screen, the home television screen, and the computer screen retain their separate locations, yet the types of images you see on each of them are losing their medium-based specificity. (Friedberg 2000: 439)

In this chapter I will be using the cinema screen, television screen and computer screen in order to, first, introduce the principal media forms to be detailed throughout this study and, second, to highlight the main points of distinction and convergence. This will also extend to 'appliances' such as VCRs, DVD players and videogame consoles. Highlighting the main historical developments, in this chapter I will also outline key industrial determinants as well as introducing the respective 'audiences' of each of the key forms, from the cinema spectator and television viewer to the computer user and videogame player.

Cinema

The largest and most apparent screen-machine in this book, cinema has nevertheless become a prime focus for arguments against what is known as technological determinism. Technological determinism is the view that technology provides its own drive, that it somehow progresses, self-propelled, in complete isolation from social, cultural and economic factors. Two histories and enquiries are available to us in this respect. First of all, how did cinema begin when it did; and second, how has cinema progressed in the way that it has? In his account of the development of photography, cinema and television, Brian Winston argues that the introduction of new technologies can never be regarded in terms of immediate and unbridled adoption and acceptance. It is in this respect that the theory of technological determinism must always be tempered by consideration of something more approaching stops and starts, external pressures and breaks, or what Winston terms 'necessities' and 'constraints' (Winston 1996: 1–9). Here, Winston responds to Andre Bazin's (1967) now famous rumination – exactly why is it that we regard 1895 as the year in which cinema was invented? Cinema has had several precedents. One might well look back on the invention of the Camera Obscura in 1553, for example, as starting the drive towards more photographic rather than painterly representations of the world. But further than that we would need to ask: why did it take four centuries for developments such as the Zoetrope (1824) and Daguerreotype (1839) to provide us with moving images? While photography does indeed help explain the pre-history of cinema as representation and the moving image its essential dynamic, Winston is much more concerned with the formation of cinema as a recognizable institution:

> What I am suggesting . . . is that particular developments in the 1890s, exemplified by the formation of cartels and unions exactly in the years of the birth of cinema (1895/6), reflect the existence of a large mass audience being served by a highly organised *and recently created* industry. (Winston 1996: 35)

Almost as soon as it had brought attention round to the mental machinery of cinema, apparatus theory also insisted that the development of cinema cannot be looked on purely in terms of technology and technique. Rather, the development of cinema must also be located within the context of industrial and, further, ideological factors (see Heath 1980; de Lauretis and Heath 1980). Far from being unleashed, therefore, technologies escape and only the ones that survive internal and external factors go on to become adopted. As Michael Allen explains, the internal development of cinema has been based on 'improvement' and 'innovation'. Improvement predominates because that development has been based on a succession of new and improving technologies rather than innovation for innovation's sake. Added to this, external factors – including competition with other media – have also ensured the gradual and even development of cinema over the past century. From initial novelty through to the digital present, cinema has rarely registered as a complete shock to the system because it has always been systematic. In short, it has evolved along with society:

> The development of any new film technology is ... grounded in its socio-economic context. Central to this argument is that any innovation and development in film technology is market-led or, at least, is in a symbiotic relationship with the market. The audience must want what the technology can provide before it succeeds and becomes naturalised. (Cook and Bernink 1999: 45)

The internal and external combine to put paid to the notion of pure, immediate and unprecedented 'firsts' in the history of film and cinema. Initially useful but ultimately too specific, the accepted canon of breakthrough films in the areas of sound, colour and widescreen – *The Jazz Singer* (1927), *Becky Sharpe* (1935) and *The Robe* (1953) – has been challenged in numerous ways. How are we to distinguish, for example, between precedents, public firsts and more accomplished successors, the films through which new technologies are generally revealed to be more than potential fads? Precedents are useful in the fact that they help put the canonical firsts into perspective, emphasizing the specificity of their claim and approaching some of the reasons why they represent such important breakthroughs. In the area of sound, for example, while *Don Juan* (1926) was the first film to make use of a synchronized soundtrack, *The Jazz Singer* does remain the first 'talkie' (however much this related only to songs and a few fragments of speech). Similarly, while *The Gulf Between* (1915) was the first film to use two-strip Technicolor, *Becky Sharpe* was the first film to make use of the more successful three-strip Technicolor. The acknowledged firsts, there-fore, must be put into perspective not only with internal reference to precedents and successors but also with a range of external factors including patents and standardization, competition and consolida-tion, and audience responses to these new technologies of the screen (see also Gomery 1980; Wollen 1980).

Looking specifically at the development of widescreen, there is first of all the fact that although appropriate processes were available in the late 1920s and early 1930s – principally the Hypergonar lens and three-camera Polyvision – it wasn't uniformly adopted until the arrival of Cinerama and CinemaScope in the 1950s. A range of tech-nical criteria and economic necessities had to be fulfilled for the more widespread implementation of this, the 'last' and largest of the main cinema technologies. In broad terms, widescreen was the response to an economic downturn in studio profits in the late 1940s and early 1950s. Where this fall in profits was only partly engen-dered by the introduction of television, studios recognized that they could only ward off further competition with the inevitable rise of its domestic competitor through the consolidated introduction of a new form of exhibition based on size and scale (see Balio 1985 and 1990; Neale 1998). The first of the new widescreen processes was Cinerama, launched in 1952 with the showcase *This is Cinerama.* Cinerama films were shot and exhibited on a three-camera, multi-projector basis. Projected onto a concave screen it provided for not only widescreen viewing but also panoramic spectacle. Primarily, however, Cinerama remained too much a special attraction. For those wanting to become engrossed in full-length feature films, its flaws included being able to see the 'join' of the cameras and only those spectators positioned in the optimum central position received the full intended effect. Mainly used for non-narrative genres such as the travelogue, essentially Cinerama proved far too cumbersome and expensive to be fully adopted by the Hollywood film industry, rely-ing not only on changes in filmmaking but also a fundamental restructuring of cinema screens and auditoria (see Belton 1988; Wollen 1993).

Benefiting from the interest surrounding Cinerama, CinemaScope was to prove far more industry- and audience-friendly; its defining advantage was that it was a complete system that combined cine-matography and projection, colour and four-track stereo sound. Providing for a very firm technical basis, the first three CinemaScope films, *The Robe, Gentlemen Prefer Blondes* (1953) and *How to Marry a Millionaire* (1953), very much exemplified the resulting attractions. A biblical epic, a musical comedy and a romantic comedy, these films offered all the now magnified essentials of epic scale, glamorous stars and Technicolor spectacle. As John Belton argues, apart from the 'material' determinants of widescreen – economics and technology – there was also a number of 'ideological' factors that helped CinemaScope succeed over rival processes Cinerama and 3D. These become most transparent in the ways in which each process was pitched to the public and received by the trade and popular press. Although referring to economic determinants of class, Belton also refers to different 'tiers' of spectator. Cinerama appealed to a non-traditional motion picture audience, the newly leisure-obsessed middle and upper-middle classes. For its part, 3D mainly helped define a 'lower' class of spectator. Launched through films such as *Bwana Devil* (1952), *House of Wax* (1953) and *It Came from Outer Space* (1953), they tended to play for cheap thrills, a lion leaping out of the screen or the alien bursting through a door towards you. Major studios ceased production of 3D films in 1954 but as further films such as *The Creature from the Black Lagoon* (1954) illustrate, 3D became associated with exploitation films sold to teenagers at drive-in theatres. Essentially, then, CinemaScope appealed to the middle ground and the majority. Getting rid of the neck and eye strain, CinemaScope offered both comfort and a now even larger-than-life escapism. In short, it renewed the norm (Belton 1988: 40–3; see also Belton 1992).

CinemaScope was effectively replaced by the less extreme Panavision in the late 1960s and other widescreen processes have included VistaVision, Todd AO and 70mm. Three of the main developments in cinema exhibition since the consolidation of widescreen have been in the areas of sound, the introduction of multiplex cinemas and, as I will be outlining in my Conclusion, the advent of digital cinema. Sound is the principal factor in turning essentially 2D viewing into a 3D experience. Following on from the introduction of Dolby Stereo in the mid-1970s, other developments such as THX and digital sound systems have worked in extending the so-called 'off-screen' space of cinema, providing sound with depth and direction enough to make audiences feel as though the action is happening all around them (see, in particular, Sergi 1998, 2001 and 2004). The growth of multiplexes since the 1980s has both added to and detracted from the special event of going to the cinema. Caught up in a total culture of consumption, and where there are more people than ever in the same building, multiplexes offer choice and comfort but often at the expense of the big screen experience. Which is to say that customers take their chances with regard to whether they get to see a blockbuster release on Screen 1 or on the much smaller Screen 13 a few weeks later. More can also be less and many screens are now actually smaller than they were in the 1970s (see Harbord 2002; Acland 2003; Jancovich, Faire and Stubbings 2003).

If both of these developments can be said to have enhanced and altered the apparatus and architecture of existing cinemas, two developments that have sought to expand the cinematic experience beyond conventional cinema viewing are so-called movie rides and IMAX. Movie rides simultaneously complicate and extend issues relating to cinematic spectacle, taking us out of cinemas and into theme parks where we are invited to enter into film worlds like never before. There is, first of all, the conventional tour around sets, as in Universal's *Jaws* and *Jurassic Park* rides where tourists are beset by animatronics and get to see live stunt sequences. Then there are attractions like Universal's *Terminator 2: 3D* and Disney's *Honey, I Shrunk the Audience* which do involve cinema screens but also live effects and motion effects. Finally, there are motion-effect simulator rides such as Disney's *Star Tours* and *Back to the Future* rides (see Darley 2000: 33–6; King 2000: 176–84; Allen 2003: 225–32). The most immediate link back to cinema is that blockbusters have themselves come to be regarded as thrill rides (see Bukatman 2003; Balides 2003; Kramer 2003). IMAX can be located in-between movie rides and conventional cinema, the screen still intact but larger than ever and wrapped up in 'The IMAX Experience'. Founded in 1970, IMAX is the modern equivalent of Cinerama in that it still remains a special attraction. Optimum viewing is theoretically available all around the custom-built theatres as spectators look up at the panoramic screen. Filmed on the equivalent of 70mm film, image quality remains clear and with advanced sound systems the overall experience is like 3D without the glasses. As Tana Wollen (1993) outlines, the particular spectacular features of IMAX mean that it has traditionally been restricted to documentary and short films celebrating travel, nature, technology and adventure. More recently, however, IMAX has proven the ideal secondary outlet for selected blockbusters such as *Apollo 13* (1995), *Star Wars* Episode II, the *Matrix* sequels and *Spider-Man 2* (2004). Developments such as IMAX and the forthcoming digital 3D prompt the latest questions about narrative and spectacle, viewing and experience. Working to extend our perceptual limits, our eyes and ears stretched to capacity, the main question, of course, is: how much can we take? This is a question, however, that's been asked since the very beginnings of cinema.

Home viewing: TV, VCRs and DVD

To move from the cinema to the home is to move to a much more private location with a greater degree of choice. The constant transmission of television programmes into people's homes has been regarded in many ways, from scheduled 'structure' and 'viewing habits' to 'flow', 'fragmentation' and 'dispersal' (see Fiske 1987; Caldwell 1995; Everett 2003). To begin with, then, where broadcast television is much more domestic and continuous, cinema remains a public place, a specific choice and a special occasion. Film Studies always seems to win in this respect, even – or especially – in those moments when Film and Television Studies tackle the same areas. And nowhere is this more evident than with the viewer. From the involved 'spectator' of big movies to the passive 'viewer' of television, and the seduced 'gaze' of the film spectator to the distracted 'glance' of the television viewer, film audiences are given the benefit of attention, fascination and focus whereas television viewers are often presented as aimless channel hoppers looking for their next quick fix of images and information (see Ellis 1982; Caldwell 1995; Stam and Shohat 2000). However, Jay David Bolter and Richard Grusin maintain that it is exactly these types of 'technological' and 'ontological' differences that have become eroded in recent years, not least through the ability to watch films on television and the development of home cinema (Bolter and Grusin 1999: 185–7). Maybe this brings us to the heart of convergence. What do film and television, respectively, gain from that erosion or is convergence simply a matter of technologies meeting in the middle? All technologies can be said to lose and gain something in this transaction. So, with regard to the main focus of this book we might ask: when transferred to the home, does film benefiting from some of the advantages of television such as immediacy and intimacy make up for the fact that there is also a reduction in scope and size?

The relationship between film and broadcast television has been one of competition and conjunction. Remaining competitive in terms of big screen versus small, conjunction can be regarded in terms of shared business practices and production values. The former ranges from major deals regarding the rights to show films on television to the conglomeration of film and television studios; and the latter including fundamental crossovers in style and genre, for example recent documentaries given a theatrical release such as *Spellbound* (2002) and *Fahrenheit 9/11* (2004), and 'cinematic' television series like *CSI* and *24*. While television sets have been widely available since the 1950s, the new is very much a matter of additionality. With particular regard to transmission, Michele Hilmes (2002) charts the influences and effects of cable, satellite and digital television, developments that have not only given us wider access to a greater range of programmes but have also come to alter fundamentally what we regard as public or even national viewing. More television has also led to the growth of film channels, ranging from the first of its kind, Home Box Office (HBO), in 1975, to the Sky Movie Channel, established in 1991. And digital television now brings pristine picture quality and assorted interactive features to both television and film viewing (see also Wasko 1994; Maltby 1995; Friedberg 2000; Monaco 2000).

The most significant addition to television sets over the past thirty years, and the one most specific to watching and re-watching films, is the video cassette recorder. VCRs can be said to have an ambiguous status between Film and New Media Studies, an analogue medium that nevertheless carries with it some of the same language of new media in terms of 'access' and 'ability'. VCRs work in intercepting and storing television transmissions, and have been said to have changed film viewing in numerous ways. With the introduction of the VCR, people are now in a position to watch their own choice of films at home. Choice is important in this respect and differs from merely watching films scheduled on television in terms of both time and availability. There is the choice of not only *what* films to watch but also *when* to watch them. And the ability to stop, fast forward, freeze frame and rewind fundamentally effects the narrative flow of films. For all theories surrounding the fluidity of digital media and the relative inertia of analogue, then, VCRs benefit from being able to capture transmissions and hold them on tape, a hard copy that is also flexible enough to be viewed, re-viewed and manipulated until degradation sets in.

Two lessons come to us from the early history of VCRs that have been variously avoided or simply repeated in the introduction of subsequent entertainment systems and are almost *de rigueur* when it comes to the competitive practices and open flow of digital media: format and copyright. Although videotape recording equipment had been in research and development since the 1950s, it wasn't until the release of the Sony Betamax recorder, the SL-7200, in 1975 that the home video revolution was born. Claimed as the first successful VCR, Matsushita and JVC nevertheless worked on their own format and introduced VHS in 1976, the first available VHS machine being JVC's HR-3300. Simply put, although Betamax resulted in better picture quality, VHS's two-hour tapes proved much more popular than Betamax's initial one-hour recording times. Other companies rushed in to adopt VHS and it soon became the industry standard. Sony turned to VHS in 1988 and the Betamax system was finally discontinued in 2002. With particular regard to copyright, in 1976 Universal and Disney sued Sony over what was, after all, the prime feature of video recorders, the ability to copy films and television programmes. Ambiguous in the extreme and rarely enforced, it wasn't until 1984 that the US Supreme Court ruled that home taping doesn't violate copyright laws. Part of that ambiguity is the fact that film companies had quickly come to follow the commercial advantages of VCRs, in effect providing another outlet for films and literally extending their shelf life in terms of rentals and purchase. In 1979, films earned 80 per cent of their receipts from theatrical release and 20 per cent from video and television. In 1985, the year that Blockbuster opened its first video store, the home video business had come to generate more revenue than theatrical rentals, and in 1993 American theatrical exhibition accounted for 20 per cent of film earnings, overseas theatrical exhibition 15 per cent and the rest television and video sales (see Wasko 1994; Maltby 1995; Friedberg 2000; Smith 2004).

As Barbara Klinger argues, 'surrogate' forms of cinema such as video-cassettes, laserdiscs and now DVDs have radically transformed the spectator's relationship to film. Effectively working in bringing cinema from out there, up on high, down to the level of a malleable commodity, the previously 'unapproachable medium that hovered in the distance on the silver screen' has been thoroughly tamed and domesticated:

Today cinema can be contained in small boxes, placed on a shelf, left on the coffee table or thrown on the floor. Spectators can pause, fast-forward, rewind or mangle images through the VCR; they can program a laserdisc player so that it shows only the desired scenes. In these alternative formats, films can be viewed repeatedly at the spectator's whim and achieve an indelible place in everyday routines. This previously remote, transitory and public medium has thus attained the solidity and semi-permanent status of a household object, intimately and infinitely subject to manipulation in the private sphere. (Klinger 2001: 133–4)

Rather than seeing this as a reduction of public into private, however, Klinger argues that there is more 'cinema' than ever before. It has become 'not only a commonplace element of leisure, but an inextricable component of everyday life' (Klinger 2001: 134).

Of all the other systems designed to provide an alternative to videotape – including the ill-fated videodisc and the relatively specialist laserdisc – only DVD has managed to forge the transition from videotape to film discs successfully. Pioneer began developing DVD in 1991, with Sony and Philips expressing an interest soon after. Partly mindful of the varying video player formats which had left numerous companies stranded in the 1970s and 1980s, the DVD Consortium was formed in 1995. What this meant was that where video succeeded regardless of competition, DVD came to being through relative consensus. Looking at the convergent nature of CDs and CD-ROMs, for example, companies had come to realize that widely varying DVD systems wouldn't succeed in taking over from video players and cassettes in the newly emergent, disc-centred, home entertainment market. Plans for a two-sided disc format, for example, were abandoned early in the process, practically speaking because neither CD compatible systems nor CD-ROM drives work through this flipsided process. Convergence also goes towards explaining use of the term, Digital Versatile Disc, as opposed to Digital Video Disc. The first DVD player, the Panasonic A-100, was released in America in 1997. Slowly spreading into other regions, DVDs first became available for rent from Blockbuster in 2001; 100 million discs were purchased in Britain alone in 2002, and by 2003 DVD had become the preferred option for both the rental and purchase of films (Smith 2004).

The rise of DVD players can't be taken in isolation from the rise of other entertainment systems and technologies. As Anne Friedberg (2002) suggests, similar parallels can be drawn with the transition from audiotape to CD in the 1980s and 1990s. The word 'transition' is important in this respect because old technologies do not just cease to exist when new technologies enter the market. There is always a relatively long period of 'phasing in' overlapping with 'phasing out', and in the case of music, while CDs currently dominate the market, audiotapes are still produced and purchased. And we are at the point now, of course, when there has been resurgence in the vinyl market and CDs have been facing stiff competition from MP3 players. Some of the same rules apply to DVDs. Where CDs and DVDs have the advantage with regard to sound quality and the ability to click – rather than wind – through tracks and scenes, we need to bear in mind the ingrained familiarity of prior forms and formats; in many respects an increased nostalgia for 'depth' of analogue sound or image and the 'authentic' crackle of an old tape or glitch in the image in the case of video. The main sticking point appears to be the fact that CD and DVD started as read-only formats. Where CDs have come to address that, and in the process got in on the act of down-loadable music with rewritable CDs, video recorders will remain a feature of the home until DVDs become recordable as standard.

The reasons for the DVD's success are numerous and convergent. We might well begin with what Barbara Klinger has termed the 'hardware aesthetic'. Highlighted through film collectors' special fondness for the laserdisc, this aesthetic refers not to the machines themselves – the sleek silver design of DVD players as opposed to the old black box effect of VCRs, for example – but the ways in which

> The value of films is often largely determined by the quality of the transfer, the aura of the digital reproduction of sound and image, and even the pristine surface of the laserdisc itself. These priorities in turn lead to a preference for certain kinds of films over others – that is, films that have visual surfaces and technical features that appear to highlight and reinforce the capabilities of digital technology. (Klinger 2001: 142)

If nostalgia for analogue forms is one thing that ensures a longer period of 'phasing out', the fetish for perfection becomes the psychological equivalent with regard to the 'phasing in' of digital products.

As Klinger concludes, however, we can't take the seduction of nice shiny discs and all that they deliver in terms of pristine images and sensuous sounds out of context of market forces. Cinema entering into the home is accompanied by another paradox, particularly when it comes to the film fan and collector:

[W]hile the world of the collector seems exclusive and personal, it is strongly influenced by discourses of media industries and their technologies. Consumption in general provides an intense link between private and public spheres (obviously, one purchases mass-produced objects so as to make them personal possessions). At the same time, media industries offer consumers the rhetorics of intimacy (i.e. 'secrets' of the cinema) and mastery (i.e. technological expertise or media knowledge) to enhance consumers' sense of owning a personalised product. (Klinger 2001: 147)

Focusing in particular on film fandom, Henry Jenkins (2000) has made the case for the cult properties of videotape; that is, the circulation and ownership of particular films and genres. The case is well made but within the context of an industry that also fostered a further consolidation of mainstream film viewing, the purchase and possession of films has the potential to make fans of us all. DVDs have come to follow the same pattern with regard to catering for 'cult' and 'mainstream' films, Hollywood and international film, and recent evidence has also suggested that people still buy big and rent small; that is, purchase blockbusters and rent lesser-known films (Richards 2002; Hewitt 2003). In many ways, then, DVDs have merely firmed up on the purchase and rental patterns established by VHS. So, apart from the obvious sense of novelty, the success of DVDs in replacing videotape must lie with innate and overriding technical factors: digitality and versatility.

First of all, DVD represents a return to the cinematic. As particularly manifest in the less-than-accommodating pan-and-scan process, video simply adapted and became reduced to television (see Neale 1998; King 2002). DVD represents a return to the cinematic in terms of the attention paid to sound and vision, the resurrection of the widescreen format, and these properties in conjunction with the technical developments of home cinema. But as well as clarity and enhancement of the viewing experience, DVDs also provide us with special features that are informational rather than cinematic and organized according to the same 'navigation' properties as film websites and satellite and digital television. Branching out from the main menu, the viewer-cum-user can choose to access commentaries, deleted scenes, documentaries and promotional material, and special interactive features such as storyboard-to-film comparisons and the ability to choose camera angles on certain scenes. Overall, then, DVDs provide us with clarity of image and density of information.

Part educational, mainly self-promotional, the special features are said to enrich the main feature by supplementing it with exclusive content (see Barker 2004; Harper 2005). Sleek and functional, DVD represents the most circumscribed convergence of the cinematic and the digital.

Computers and the internet

To move from the television screen to computers is to move to a once impersonal medium now regarded in intimate terms. The previously scientific and indeed science fiction nature of computers has been softened by the widespread adoption of the personal computer. And while we might still refer to VDUs or, more likely, computer monitors, the 'computer screen' more accurately reflects where we are now with regard to what we see and do on that screen, and the life that takes place behind and beyond it. Although computers are less central to homes than television and are still in many ways associated with work or working from home, our personal association with PCs begins with privacy of place. Bracketed off from the television in the living room, we sit much closer to this smaller screen and there is also a very tactile connection as we type away on the keyboard or slide and click the mouse. Certainly, computerization has become much more ubiquitous in recent years. We can now access, organize and interact with information on digital television, iPods, palm pilots and mobile phones. But as a definite focus, still and some time yet to come the predominant means of access to computer-mediated information and communication, the PC screen is where the self becomes networked in the most sustained and concentrated fashion.

Beginning with comparisons and contrasts between cinema and computers, there are obvious differences in terms of size and activity. With regard to actual content, while cinema is essentially a sight-and-sound medium, the main distinction is that modern computers are also a *textual* medium. Whether created in document form or experienced as a psychedelic wave of scrolling chat, however, words on the computer screen also work in making text a dynamic visual form, documents malleable until a hard copy is printed out and chat taking on a hyperactive life of its own. Looking at what he terms the 'cultural interface', Lev Manovich warns of looking at the three modes of modern computer culture – text, image and activity – in separate spheres. It is in this respect that he is able to look at the printed word, cinema and the human–computer interface (HCI) in terms of the 'human–computer–culture-interface – the ways in which computers present and allow us to interact with cultural data' (Manovich 2001: 70). In terms of the history of cinema and computers, one mistake is to regard the latter as new and solely functional. As Manovich details their parallel histories, both the Daguerreotype and Charles Babbage's Analytical Engine were designed in the 1830s, and computing also came into practice in the formative decade of cinema through Herman Hollerith's Tabulator Machine used for key census data in the 1890s. Although we have come to regard cinema as a bona fide medium rather than a technology, both forms rely on 'recorded' data that is then 'read', film recorded on camera and played through a projector and software via a database and through the hardware. Only recently has the computer progressed from mathematical machine to become an all-round 'media synthesizer and manipulator' (Manovich 2001: 21–6).

Parallel histories also lead to parallel formal developments. As Per Persson argues, early cinema can be said to have shared many properties with primitive computing, properties that make recent convergence between the two forms inevitable or at least not so surprising. Focusing on the subject of space, Persson outlines cinema's original transfer of 'theatrical space' onto an initially very limited 'screen space'. Which is to say that early silent films were merely composed of vaudeville-style performances taking place against flat backdrops and with the fixed camera able to do little but photograph long takes. The same stillness can be seen in the emergence of the Graphical User Interface (GUI) in the 1950s and 1960s, where a static 'camera' was used to frame basic desktop applications. The developments from thereon in follow editing, narrative, camera movement and so on within cinema, and digital environments in computing where simulation combines with depth and the illusion of movement and navigation is enabled by the mobile camera. This is where the computer screen is given a film 'frame' and, paramount for both media, the suggestion of 'off-screen space'. But this is still not to forget the insurmountable differences between cinema and computers, which Persson ultimately sees as belonging to the user:

> Digital space . . . is a *performative* space; it includes many objects with endless and complex possible connections and relations between them,

the importance of which depends on the momentary purpose of the user
... The *narrative* function of cinema and the *tool* function of digital
space place radically different requirements on the design of these
spaces. As cinema *spectators* we have to understand space, but as
computer *users* we both have to understand and *act* within digital space,
and that makes things more complicated. (Persson 2001: 52)

The personal computer first entered into people's homes in the
1980s. A tool for basic programming and gaming, it wasn't until the
advent of the World Wide Web in the 1990s, however, that computers came to be regarded as part of a fully fledged medium: the internet. From military origins and academic development through to its
use in business and entertainment, the internet has developed
through numerous stages. The tendency of Cyberculture Studies in
approaching the history of the internet has been to think big. Two of
the most familiar stories in this respect are the US Department of
Defense's Advanced Research Projects Agency, which engineered
the ARPANET in the late 1960s, and William Gibson's coining of the
term 'cyberspace' in his influential 1984 cyberpunk novel,
Neuromancer. With military origins on the one side and the cyberpunk sensibility on the other, throughout the 1990s the internet was
regarded as a place of commerce and surveillance on the one hand
and a wide open space for freedom of information and communication on the other (see, for example, Jordan 1999; Bell 2001). The
tendency of New Media Studies, however, has been to pull back and
look at the forgotten moments in the development of the internet, the
actual mechanisms as opposed to the conspiracy thriller or science
fiction narratives. There is, for example, Vannevar Bush's work on
the Memex in the 1930s and 1940s, and Ted Nelson's Project
Xanadu which, although never completed, led to the coining of the
term 'hypertext' in 1963. As Jeremy G. Butler explains, the fundamental protocols of the internet were in place by 1982. The current
market version of the internet, the World Wide Web, first came into
being in 1990 and 1991. Originally designed as a hypertext-based
'information mesh', designer Tim Berners-Lee went on to create 'the
two basic building blocks of the Web', the exchange protocol and
text conventions enabled by hypertext transfer protocol (HTTP) and
hypertext markup language (HTML). It wasn't until the introduction
of web browsers – principally Mosaic in 1993, Netscape in 1994 and
Microsoft's Internet Explorer in 1995 – however, that the Web was
to become the 'killer application' of its time (Butler 2002: 40–3).

As much as distinctions can be made within this most remediating of forms, the internet provides for information and content. Narrowing the search down to entertainment, for example, the internet can be used for accessing information regarding media and popular culture, and has increasingly become an alternative outlet for accessing content in the form of news stories, magazine features, and downloadable films and television programmes. The information potential of the internet has always been apparent in its use of text and images. We can only begin to speak of actual content, however, by looking at the 'plug-ins' that have allowed users to access audio and video. Beginning with RealNetworks' RealPlayer in 1995, and quickly followed by Apple's QuickTime and Microsoft's Windows Media Player, streaming delivery and the ability to download audio and video material have made the internet both a comparable and yet still notably distinct medium from radio and television. Given the technical limitations of early plug-ins – thumb-nail clips and relatively poor sound and video prone to constant buffering – writing in 2002, Butler sees the crossover between cinema and the internet as much more potential than actual. Successful in terms of web radio and downloadable music, the internet has not yet been able to compete with television or cinema to a significant extent, instead allowing for new and alternative forms such as short films, music videos, animation, online gaming, pornography and webcam sites. As Butler argues, the overriding difference is that while television and film are fundamentally 'push' media, the internet is essentially a 'pull' medium. That is, while film and television are almost entirely predicated around viewing, the internet is much more about activity, the first task being to trawl through relevant sites rather than having them simply appear before you (Butler 2002: 43–7).

The computer user has not been theorized in as concentrated and accumulative a fashion as the film spectator, television viewer and videogame player. The most useful continuity between Cyberculture and New Media Studies has been the consideration of online identities. Often curbed in terms of mind and body, the familiar image is that of the computer user with their back to the world and eyes to the screen. Leaving their solitary body behind, the mind is effectively transported through the screen into a 'consensual hallucination' where identity is free and flexible (see Rheingold 1993; Turkle 1997; McPherson 2002; Lister *et al.* 2003: 166–76; Peters 2003). The main difficulty is in imagining a single computer user engaged in as diverse a set of operations as word-processing to surfing the Net. Following on from the cinematic 'gaze' and televisual 'graze', several terms have been suggested for multimedia. Myra MacDonald (2000), for example, has suggested the 'flit'. Carrying familiar connotations of fidgety distraction, nevertheless the 'flit' attempts to match eye with act, and while we do take in more information to less effect, there is at least the potential for accessing more information about particular subjects. Focusing more specifically on convergence, Dan Harries suggests the 'viewser', a term that combines the essential properties of seeing and doing:

> 'Viewsers' are the new 'connected consumers' who find entertainment pleasure in the multitasking activities being promoted through their computer and television screens. In other words, entertainment value is not only measured by what they see and hear, but also by what they do and the ways in which their activities have a direct impact on a developing narrative. (Harries 2002b: 172)

This combination of viewing and activity is, indeed, a defining characteristic of convergence, especially in those cases where a narrative is played out across multiple media. The particular trick here is to put activity to use, existing not merely as an automatic pleasure in its own right but also having an input into and effect upon the central text.

Videogames and players

A number of distinctions arise when approaching the formal study of videogames. Following on from the increasingly interactive viewers of cinema and television, and the multitasking users of PCs, videogames require players. Previously dismissed as a waste of time – a childish distraction from, if not dangerous addition to life – in recent years playing videogames has come to be regarded in terms of complexity and skill, in many ways a much more concentrated and involved connection between participant and screen than computing. Secondly, the history of videogames has progressed through much more explicit consideration of hardware, not merely the player's hands-on control over the events on screen but also the different and developing forms of videogame systems. Difference refers to the three main forms of videogame, each of which presents us with varying screens, can be found in contrasting locations, and requires its own unique methods of control. Where 'videogame' has become the generic name for all such forms of 'electronic' or 'computer' games since the early 1970s (see Wolf 2001a; Wolf and Perron 2003a), arcade, computer and console games put the player in altogether different situations. In terms of both size and subsequent activity, arcade machines represent the most apparent and public form of videogame hardware. Of the three forms, however, I would make the case for consoles representing the ideal focus. Arcade gaming may well bring us closer to comparisons with cinema understood in terms of size and experience, but severely reduce the narrative dimension of film. Conversely, computer games represent the most specialist and private form of gaming. Because of the various sound and graphics cards required for PCs, the computer gamer still remains something of a hobbyist. And this also applies to the types of games available for PCs. Although there is significant overlap, computer games have traditionally been seen as more complex and refined than those offered by consoles. Console games, however, provide us with the cinematic-experiential *and* the film-textual, the size obviously reduced when compared with arcade games but often allowing us to play cinematic games on the television screen. Console games are also regarded as much more commercial and generic than computer games. Finally, then, console games bring us closer to comparisons with the Hollywood film industry. This refers to both the hardware and the software, the former comparable to VCRs and DVD players and the latter with relevant aspects of film production and promotion.

Games companies gain most of their revenue from software. The hardware is the initial marketing hook, a one-off purchase in an economy – characteristic of the post-industrial economy as a whole – where software represents a continual flow of purchases. The importance of successive consoles gaining a foothold in the home market is, however, supremely important. The first Home Video Game System was the Magnavox Odyssey, released in 1972. It wasn't until the company that brought us the first successful arcade game, *Pong* (1972), released the Atari Video Computer System 2600 in 1977, however, that videogames started to become a regular feature of families' homes. The infiltration of these and subsequent game systems into the home cannot be taken in isolation from other trends and technologies. Atari's domestic success, for example, coincided with the introduction of VCRs and the arcade boom of the late 1970s. But this can also work the other way round and, partly unable to compete with the introduction of microcomputers, Atari became a victim of the 'great video game industry crash' of 1984. It was left to two Japanese companies, Nintendo and Sega, to dominate the videogame market in the 1980s and early 1990s. Nintendo successfully redefined the market with the introduction of its 8-bit Famicom (Family Computer) in Japan in 1983 and its subsequent release as the Nintendo Entertainment System (NES) in the US in 1985. Following similar lines to Atari, Nintendo had proven itself with the success of an arcade game, *Donkey Kong* (1980), but unlike endless variations of *Pong* was then able to extract the plumber character and build a series of adventures and all-round mascot in the form of Mario. Aimed squarely at the child and family market, and armed with aggressive advertising and multimedia opportunities, by 1990 one third of American homes were in possession of a NES (see Kinder 1991; Sheff 1993; Kent 2001). Assisted by its own mascot, Sonic the Hedgehog, and aiming more at the child and teen market, Sega released its 8-bit Sega Master System in 1986 and the 16-bit Sega Genesis System – renamed the Sega Megadrive in the UK – in 1989. Having taken time out to release its highly successful Game Boy, Nintendo went on to consolidate its lead with the release of the 16-bit Super NES (SNES) in 1991.

The release of new games consoles has led to further collateral in what have been termed the 'console wars' (see Sheff 1993; Herz 1997; Sheff and Eddy 1999; Poole 2000). On one level the progressive battles can be traced through the advances in graphics, sound and subsequent gameplay promised by successive 8-bit advances. But design, marketing and timing are also key. Soon after the release of the 32-bit Sega Saturn in 1995, the music company Sony went on to launch the Sony PlayStation. Dressed in black, aimed at the teen and twenty-something market, and finding an unofficial mascot in the form of Lara Croft, Sony went on to establish a seemingly unstoppable lead in the console market. The Nintendo 64 did little to dent Sony's domination upon its release in 1996 and the three main companies soon went on to focus on the 'next generation' battle. The 128-bit Sega Dreamcast was released in 1999, Sony's PlayStation 2 in 2000 and, soon after Microsoft's entry into the console market with its Xbox, the Nintendo GameCube in 2001. The 128-bit revolution is notable for a number of factors beyond technical specifications and the ways in which new-and-improved capabilities translated to better games. Partly due to the fact that this period saw the release of four 'superconsoles' and the fact that the videogame industry now receives more attention than ever before, what distinguishes the current state of play, most of all, is that interest in hardware has almost superseded interest in the actual games. With the qualification that the launch of new consoles represents a particularly concentrated flurry of activity and that the respective companies only succeed by supplying their consoles with successful games, reporting on specifications and capabilities has been joined by equal consideration of design and function. The 128-bit consoles, for example, are far more convergent than their predecessors, variously offering basic internet and email access, DVD compatibility and access to online gaming. That is, they now exist as much more than games machines.

Approaching the subject of videogame players, a number of key distinctions need to be established. We have already released the body from the cinema auditorium. It's now sitting at home operating hand to eye. The videogame player can be distinguished in terms of: (i) situation, (ii) the interface, and (iii) agency. Situation starts with location and extends to the particular type of gaming experience. As stated above, this might refer to arcade gaming on the one hand and the PC player on the other. With particular regard to the console gamer, it can also be used to distinguish between solitary play in the bedroom or a number of participants involved in a multiplayer game in the living room, for example. The interface refers to the connection between player, hardware and screen. This translates into physical control and agency carries that through to the player's physical control over, and psychological investment in the actual game text. As Steven Poole states, 'the videogame is not simply a cerebral or visual experience; just as importantly it is a physical involvement – the tactile success or otherwise of the human-machine interface' (Poole 2000: 73). The player's main connection with machine and game is through the controller, the once monstrous joystick now transformed into the dextrous joypad. Most joypads such as Sony's Dual Shock controller and Nintendo's Rumble Pack also allow for basic force feedback; that is, vibrations ranging from subtlety of movement to the more explicit exchange of gunfire. Other peripherals tend to be genre-specific, such as steering wheels for driving games, lightguns for shoot-'em-ups and recent innovations such as the dance mat and eye toy. Looking to the future of videogaming, Poole pulls short of domestic systems that might offer the same effect as arcade gaming or fully immersive VR. Such developments might actually '*narrow* the field of possibilities', simultaneously limiting games to walking and shooting, and denying us the 'pleasurable unreality of human-body physics' as evidenced in the jumping and somersaulting adventures of Lara Croft. Poole is justifiably conservative on this matter:

> Counter-intuitively, it seems for the moment that the perfect videogame 'feel' requires the ever-increasing imaginative and physical involvement of the player to stop somewhere short of full bodily immersion. After all, a sense of pleasurable control implies some modicum of *separation*: you are apart from what you are controlling. You don't actually want to *be* there. (Poole 2000: 77)

The greater or more unwieldy the interface, the more limited the sense of agency. Although game peripherals are designed to become a transparent and natural part of the gaming process, agency refers to the wholly invisible connection between player and screen. Both technical and psychological, it completes the circuit from essentially passive body to the often impossibly active game characters on screen. In effect, it refers to the player *in* the game. So, the physical aspect of gaming is only apparent when mastering the controls of a new game. Once mastery has been achieved, the physical merges into the background. Interactivity becomes habitual and it is not so much that the physical aspect has become unimportant as the fact that it has become part of the overall flow of the gaming experience. This ongoing synthesis between player, system and game is an essential part of the much valued 'difficulty curve' or 'tilt' of videogames. The success or otherwise of the curve is dependent on retaining the player's sense of involvement throughout the course of the entire game. Practice levels are entirely predicated around the player getting used to control systems, and difficulty curves work through the gradual increase in the skills required to progress through the game. Agency therefore takes over from the inherent technical limitations of videogames. These not only apply to players finding out that they are taking part in pre-determined narratives unfolding in circumscribed spaces but also the fact that actual physical control is both incongruous and restricted. Buttons are not limbs and the same buttons are often used, in the same way, for wildly different operations such as opening a door and shooting a gun. Andrew Darley sees these restrictions as being most apparent in role-playing games (RPGs). It is principally action games – so-called 'twitch' games – that provide for the most immediate balance of skill, sensation and the illusion of taking part in acts of spectacular risk. This 'vicarious kinaesthesia' is a fundamental part of the process that, in effect, compensates for the technical limitations of current videogames and videogame systems (Darley 2000: 155–7). To dismiss narrative-based games such as RPGs and film adaptations, however, is to dismiss agency in association with a more complete immersion. In these cases agency becomes the active and interactive equivalent of film viewing, allowing for the direct entry into, and subsequent participation in game worlds that also provide players with involved characters and stories (see Wolf and Perron 2003b; Morris 2002; Chesher 2004). From cinema and television through to computers and videogames, we have always been prone to illusions and information but have increasingly come to take a more active role in the ongoing process.

2 Digital film

The digital has been theorized in immensely fluid terms. This is based on the practical understanding that digital processes work through intricate sequences and seeming endless combinations of binary code. Or, founded upon what Nicholas Negroponte has termed the 'DNA of Information' (Negroponte 1995: 11–20), digital processes have entered into not only the body but also the genetic makeup of existing media forms. The terms most commonly applied from out of this effervescent reformation include 'manipulability', 'conversion', 'versatility' and 'interactivity'. But one of the main effects of the digital is that it has also given retrospective strength to the familiar properties of analogue in terms of 'permanence', 'authenticity', 'depth' and 'truth' (see Usai 2001; Dixon 2003).

In this chapter, I will begin by looking at the basic advantages and disadvantages of the digital image as applied to photography and film. This will be followed by consideration of digital practices in key areas of film production such as sound and editing. In the second section, I will go on to look at recent arguments surrounding 'independent' versus 'mainstream' production, beginning with the ways in which digital video has primarily been said to have benefited experimental and independent filmmaking. The most recent development, however, has been that of high-definition (HD) cameras, and filmmakers now have a variety of choices regarding which format they choose – whether film, video, digital video or high-definition. In my case studies, I will be looking at Mike Figgis's experimental *Timecode* and the DV horror films, *My Little Eye* and *28 Days Later*.

Going digital

As Timothy Binkley argues, three of the main advantages of digital media are: 'conversion', 'resilience' and 'interactivity'. First of all, analogue media work through 'transcription'. Whether ink on paper, sound on vinyl or light on film, once transcribed, analogue signals remain permanently imprinted on the receiving medium. Data from a digital source, however, is effectively stored and available for an array of uses within the receiving medium or, indeed, to be further converted to other media (Binkley 1993: 94–101). Second, one chip in the wrong place on a sculpture or too many scratches on a vinyl record, and analogue media can suffer permanent physical damage. Even where the same could happen with digital media – the computer going wrong or a scratch on a DVD – the data doesn't simply disappear, the essential source unrecoverable. Similarly, while analogue media often work through the ability to tape music and films, the more the copies, the more the reduction in quality. Data is there to be endlessly manipulated and converted in digital media, and doesn't suffer the same 'generation loss' (Binkley 1993: 101–3). And finally, Binkley sees in the spatial properties of digital media new forms of representation and involvement. It is in this sense that Binkley regards digital media in terms of 'dialogue' rather than 'monologue', the play-and-receive properties of analogue media replaced by a greater interplay between the user-creator and digital forms (Binkley 1993: 116–19). This can be applied to a number of activities from graphic design to playing videogames and downloading music compilations.

The digital image

The relative pros and cons of the digital have found particular focus as applied to the digital image. These will be explored in relation to still images and then the moving image. As Janet Harbord argues, the shift from analogue to digital can be theorized via further distinctions between 'modernism and postmodernism, the bounded and the fluid, the fixed and the ephemeral' (Harbord 2002: 139). Digital images provide us with practical and relatively 'settled' examples of digital processes in that they are the impermanent results of those processes. To begin with digital photography: as well as the usual analogue viewfinder, digital cameras contain an LCD screen. Allowing the user to hold the camera at a distance, the digital screen also allows instant viewing of the photos taken. This leads to relatively little wastage as pictures can be viewed and chosen on-screen. Stored on the camera's memory card, digital photos can then be converted onto the PC. This allows the user to edit and manipulate the images on screen: alter their size, clean them up in terms of brightness and contrast, or add effects and patterns. Once stored on the PC, digital photos can be set as screensavers, sent by email or posted on webpages. And, ultimately, the user might also want to print the pictures, whether through a photo-quality printer, emailed to their service provider's picture service or through a traditional photo-processing outlet.

The possible disadvantages of the digital might already be apparent from the above sketch of what many regard as being the hyper-convenient nature of digital cameras (and, even more so, mobile phone cameras). Digital photographs can be flexible bordering on disposable, the amount of pictures taken providing for a quantity rather than quality of images. This is further compounded by the virtual nature of so many digital photos that are not made into actual prints and what many regard to be the artificial nature of digital images. Lacking material depth and infinitely manipulable, the 'art' and 'aura' of the analogue photograph are lost along with long-standing notions of photographic 'authenticity' and 'truth'. Memories are now more like snatches of activity and can, in any case, be cleaned up after the event. And where photography has traditionally been regarded as amateur and democratic, it is now restricted to 'prosumers' (see Mitchell 1992; Lister 1995; Stallabrass 1996: 13–39).

When applied to film, the binary of analogue and digital follows in similar terms of fixity and flux but as applied to the on-going history of the moving image. Having established some of the main advantages and disadvantages of the digital image, the continuity approach to both photography and film looks at the digital image more in terms of historical evolution rather than the shock of the new. This is particularly manifest in Philip Rosen's account of the history and historicity of cinema; that is, the ways in which cinema has developed and the ways in which those developments have been theorized. In Rosen's account, claims for the radical novelty of the digital image can be put into perspective by pulling back on ecstatic accounts of the free-floating image favoured by advocates of the 'digital utopia'. Where theorists of the analogue – or 'indexical' – image such as Andre Bazin and Roland Barthes fixated on light-sensitive chemicals, proponents of the digital image fetishize maths (Rosen 2001: 305). If the numerical bases of the digital represented a complete rescuing of the image from physical referents, however, the digital image would remain purely abstract. Hence, Rosen argues that the digital, in effect, *simulates* the analogue and *mimics* photography, film and television. Or, to put it another way, the digital image still has to be an image of something. Rosen goes on to look at over-enthusiastic discourses surrounding the digital at all levels of film production, distribution and exhibition. With regard to the supposed 'infinite malleability' (Rosen 2001: 340) of the digital image, for example, Rosen quite rightly points out that, once released, digital films become just as permanent as analogue films.

Digital production

In its purest form, the digital image translates to what we actually see in print and on screen. Before we look at the ways in which this applies to the digital video image and then spectacular special-effects images (see Chapter 3), there are also the ways in which digital practices work within film production. Two of the foremost digital film practices have been in the areas of sound and editing. Sound designers such as Walter Murch and Ben Burtt have been working on 'electronic' recording and mixing since the 1970s. Developing an extensive library of sound effects, the storage capacities of the digital mean that all of these sounds are available in the one place at the same time. The sound effects can then be manipulated and combined, and filtered and channelled to give them depth and direction. Principally, digital sound practices have been said to enhance the 'worldizing' properties of contemporary film, creating more complete, three-dimensional environments (see Ondaatje 2002). The *spatial* advantages of digital processes have also come to transform the temporal art of editing. As sound designer and film editor Walter Murch states, 1995 was a watershed year in editing, the last time the number of mechanically edited films equalled the number of digital (Murch 2001: xi). The three main digital editing systems are Avid, Apple's Final Cut Pro and Microsoft's Lightworks. Murch highlights two of the main advantages of digital editing systems as being 'virtual assembly' and 'instant random access'. Unlike the 'destructive' analogue, the virtual assembly allows editors to edit sequences continuously because it is a process that separates images and information (Murch 2001: 81–2). Instant random access means that the editor can work on any part of a film at any time. Combining both of these elements, digital editing brings production and postproduction closer together in that the editing can take place as soon as the day's rushes are available, the process remaining open, as always, until the final print (Murch 2001: 107–9).

Digital editing is also referred to as non-linear editing (NLE). Digital editing's ability to work out of sequence has been used to further arguments surrounding the loss of cohesion of contemporary film narratives. As Monica Mak argues, however, digital editing still ends up 'continuity editing' when it comes to the final film text and even more so in the case of blockbusters that make use of separate production units (Mak 2003: 43–5). The most recent development in digital editing has been that of '3D editing', the ability to edit within rather than solely across frames. This has resulted in an 'Avid aesthetic' (Griffiths 2003: 19) evidenced in films such as *Requiem for a Dream* (2000), *The Rules of Attraction* (2002) and even *Hulk* (2003), each of which makes notable use of split-screen techniques. The overall 'layering' effect of 3D editing also means that actors can be moved to another part of the frame rather than entire scenes having to be re-shot. And it is also used in special-effects sequences where further perspective is required between virtual backdrops and upfront spectacle. Blurring the distinction between production and postproduction, director and editor, in total, digital editing enhances the claim that films are either made or undone in the editing suite.

Regarded in such practical terms, Janet Harbord distances herself from overarching 'historical' and 'theoretical' accounts of digital processes by looking at 'cultural' and 'industrial' applications; that is, at particular aspects of worldwide film production. She does so by focusing on two films released in 1999, the assumed blockbuster *The Matrix* and the ostensible independent film, *Run Lola Run*. While both have been read extensively in terms of digital culture – in particular their use of videogame-style techniques (see Chapter 5) – up close and beyond superficial consideration of genre, they are of course very different films. As Harbord argues:

> [T]here are significant differences between the texts that locate them within different film cultures, an argument that problematizes the

concept of digital culture as transforming film production in general terms. Technological transformations may be used across different contexts of production, but each context brings to bear the history of that paradigm. (Harbord 2002: 143)

Harbord regards *The Matrix* as 'hypertextual' and *Run Lola Run* as 'intertextual'. Providing for polished special effects, continuity editing and a linear narrative, *The Matrix* is wholly designed to take viewers into its world. Playing with different film and video formats, *Run Lola Run* has sharp visible cuts between live action and animation; and continually stopping and restarting, we never settle into one consistent narrative. The film is intertextual in that it is well aware of its philosophical content and its own textual status in this respect. *The Matrix* may well comment on notions of reality but also presents viewers with a much more attractive hyperreality (Harbord 2002: 143–6). Harbord's choice of films is useful in that they also lead to complications in the ostensible distinction between 'independent' and 'mainstream' films. An assumed Hollywood product, *The Matrix* was also an Australian co-production and more of an unheralded rather than calculated blockbuster (see Chapter 6). And while *Run Lola Run* is an ostensibly independent German film, it was also an international – or 'crossover' – success, a love story and crime thriller that combines elements of animation, music and videogames.

From DV to HD

'Independent' and 'mainstream' are, of course, loaded terms, the former privileged in terms of talented filmmakers working on low budgets to establish a distinct artistic vision, in opposition to commercial studio products that work through predictable narratives driven by stars and spectacle designed to appeal to large audiences. In the US context, independence refers to those films that are produced without financial backing from the major studios (see Lewis 1998; King 2005). This is complicated somewhat by independent films that go on to be distributed by major Hollywood studios and the assumption that all non-US and English-speaking films automatically qualify as independent or 'arthouse' films. More consistent, however, are the ways in which independent films have been characterized in terms of their use of formats other than 35mm film: namely video, 16mm and digital video. Of these, 35mm became the accepted standard for major feature film production after the 'lower-quality' 16mm had been sidelined to documentaries and newsreels in the 1930s and 1940s (see Winston 1996; Enticknap 2005). With its 'truthful' speed of 24 **frames per second** and 'correct' **aspect ratio** of 1.37, 35mm is the accepted Academy format for feature film production. With its slower frame rates and television-style aspect ratio of 1.33, 16mm film became the favoured alternative format of independent directors in the 1950s and 1960s. This was particularly evident in the 'nouvelle vague' of the period. Supremely character-ized by Jean-Luc Godard's *A Bout de Souffle (Breathless)* (1959) and François Truffaut's *Jules et Jim* (1962), the French New Wave opposed mainstream Hollywood production as particularly manifest in big-budget widescreen epics. Not adverse to borrowing from the pulp verve of American film noir, the New Wave represented a back-to-basics filmmaking which eschewed the 35mm Technicolor standard in favour of 16mm black-and-white. Rejecting expensive sets and industrial-strength hardware, this was filmmaking on a more immediate and intimate scale, often taking place on the streets and favouring naturalistic performances shot from numerous unspecified perspectives. Challenging the tidy narratives and composed frames of classical Hollywood cinema, the New Wave also made use of semi-improvised techniques such as irregular angles and jump-cut editing (see Bordwell 1985; Marie 2002; Neupert 2003).

Since the late 1960s, independent filmmakers have also had access to the further reality format of video. With speeds of anywhere between 60 and 25 frames per second, since the 1990s digital video has worked in simultaneously strengthening and refin-ing the independent-versus-mainstream argument. Which is to say that, regarded in opposition to the increasing use of digital processes in contemporary Hollywood cinema, DV opened up the potential for filmmaking of a 'comparative' yet noticeably low-budget nature. As Holly Willis suggests, from digital video onwards, the distinction between film and video has become hard to maintain (Willis 2005: 4). This refers not only to Hollywood's appropriation of DV but also to our own ability to make 'desktop' films.

Dogme

Accounts of DV tend to begin with the Dogme 95 movement. In what has been loosely termed the New New Wave, Dogme's famous 'Vow of Chastity' makes clear the similarity in intent but differences in approach to the original nouvelle vague: 'In 1960 enough was enough! The movie had been cosmeticised to death, they said; yet since then the use of cosmetics has exploded' (von Trier and Vinterberg 1995a). Where the French New Wave is said to have failed because of its 'bourgeois romanticism', the Denmark-based Dogme 95 saw itself as strictly avant-garde, redirecting the technological democratization of cinema through the strength of the group. The Vow of Chastity has ten commandments:

(1)   Filming must be done on location.
(2)   Sound and image must be produced together rather than through recourse to postproduction.
(3)   The camera must be handheld.
(4)   The film must be in colour and special lighting is not acceptable.
(5)   Optical work and filters are forbidden.
(6)   The film must not contain 'superficial action'.
(7)   Temporal and geographical alienation are forbidden, the films taking place in the 'here and now'.
(8)   Genre movies are not acceptable.
(9)   The film format must be 35mm.
(10) The director must not be credited. (von Trier and Vinterberg 1995b)

The movement was unleashed upon the world through the success of the first two Dogme films, Thomas Vinterberg's *Festen (The Celebration)* and Lars von Trier's *Idioterne (The Idiots)*, at the Cannes film festival in 1998. Followed by contributions from the two other founding members, Soren Kragh-Jacobsen's *Mifune's Sidste Sang (Mifune's Last Stand)* (1999) and Kristian Levring's *The King is Alive* (1999), further films have come from Argentina, Korea and all over Europe. The first American entry was Harmony Korine's *Julien Donkey-Boy* (1999) and to date there have been thirty-seven Dogme films, the most recent being the British entry, Jan Dunn's *Gypo* (2005).

The advantages of DV, the format of choice for the Dogme film-makers who quickly ignored their own 35mm rule, relate to production and effect. Where mainstream cinema is said to take full advantage of digital's ability to fake and manipulate the perceived reality of the photographic image, DV brings immediacy and authenticity back into the process. Location shooting releases Dogme films from the restrictions of the custom-built studio and the handheld nature of the cameras means that they can be anywhere, at any distance and often in multiple locations. This also impacts upon performance in the sense that the actors are no longing playing to camera. Two particular elements of DV filmmaking are worth looking at in more detail: film form and aesthetics. Where the digital image is often said to provide for clarity, it is also extremely versatile in being able to pick up on natural light in an almost impressionistic manner. The digital video image has been characterized in some of the same ways as the video image, in terms of 'blur' and 'grain' but also in terms of this extra-sensitivity, the camera either pre-programmed to catch the light in certain ways or enhanced after the fact in order to convey a particular aesthetic effect. This can be seen in the opening to *Festen*. The film's central character walks down a sunny country road. The effect is one of a yellow, bleached heat. This is subsequently countered by the clinical light and tomb-like darkness of the family gathering in the mansion, a celebration that becomes more like a wake. The darkness later takes an impressionistic turn as a haunted atmosphere is evoked through candlelight and mirrors. With particular regard to formal composition, DV filmmakers are prone to avoid traditional framing and take advantage of the mobile properties of digital video cameras. This is more like catching the action on the run. Although relatively contained in the mansion scenes within *Festen*, the camera combines form and content by having the camera 'sneak' around; roaming rooms and peeking round doors as the viewer assumes the position of an invisible invitee, as curious as the other guests to unearth the family's hidden secrets. This takes much more of an anarchic turn in *Idioterne* as the viewer becomes more of a participant in the group's activities. In effect, the camera also 'spazzes out' and on occasions spirals out of control the more the 'normals' in the film forget who they are (see also Schepelern 2000; Chaudhuri 2005).

Variety

Like 16mm and analogue video before it, a number of alternative orthodoxies have come to surround the use of DV. Where Hollywood's reality has traditionally resulted from colour, clarity and careful composition, the reality of independent film is that of the shaky camera and the black-and-white or blurred image. In short, where Hollywood ultimately provides for a sort of glamorous hyperreality, the 'true' reality favoured by independent filmmakers is messy and off-colour. Such is the dominance of mainstream film, however, that the reality fostered by independent film is regarded as alternative and artistic. But are we truly at the stage where DV can be said to have replaced 16mm and analogue video as the low-budget alternative to 35mm film? This is where we start to qualify the situation. The Internet Movie Database (imdb.com), for example, currently lists over 800 DV entries (January 2005). Notable DV films outside the Dogme movement include *Chuck and Buck* (2000), *Open Water* (2003) and *9 Songs* (2004). Characterized in terms of immediacy and authenticity, DV has also become the main format for recent documentary films such as *Touching the Void* (2003) and *Super Size Me* (2004). The number of IMDb entries relating to TV and short films, however, makes it difficult to ascertain an official number of feature films. DV has proven versatile rather than dominant. From a strictly amateur perspective, the availability of DV, mini DV and software packages such as Avid and Windows Movie Maker have provided for more complete production systems than Super 8 in the 1960s, Hi 8 in the 1980s and camcorders in the 1990s. And, from this amateur base, DV has come to be used in numerous other forms and outlets, whether short films, music videos, internet films or the 'new avant-garde' of multimedia installation artists and video DJs. There is a definite DV culture at work here, fostered by initiatives such as Next Wave Films and festivals such as ResFest (see Griffiths 2003; Hanson 2003; Willis 2005).

With particular regard to feature films, therefore, DV has more correctly added the *choice* of another film format. That is, we are currently at an exciting transitional phase where filmmakers are making use of video, film or digital video, and often in combination with each other. Although this might appear to pull back on the distinctive qualities of DV, it also locates digital video within the current context of film itself becoming increasingly digital. We are at the stage right now, for example, where analogue film can be committed to a digital intermediate which allows it to be run through digital editing and colour grading before the transfer back to 35mm. It is in this sense that while certain films such as *The Last Broadcast* (1998), *Pi* (1998) and *Run Lola Run* are erroneously used in accounts of DV, it's understandable why (see, for example, Griffiths 2003). *The Last Broadcast* and its more successful cousin, *The Blair Witch Project* (1999), are generally caught up in the reality effect attributed to DV, an assumption that arises from the fact that DV is also, essentially, video (both of these films made use of a combination of Hi-8 video and 16mm film). Similarly, the 16mm *Pi* and the combined 16mm and 35mm *Run Lola Run* are films that made extensive use of digital postproduction.

High-definition

The most recent development in digital cinematography is **high-definition**. Although the two terms are often confused and simply conflated, high-definition would not be possible without digital *compression*. This applies to television as much as film in that compression refers to the quantity, quality and speed of data – leading to clarity of image in terms of film, for example, and speed and clarity in terms of television transmission. Read mainly in terms of Hollywood fighting back against the use of digital video by independent filmmakers, high-definition is the generic name for professional-standard cameras that take advantage of the versatility of digital film but enable a resolution and depth of field similar to 35mm. The progressive systems have been: HDDV, DVCAM, DVC Pro, HDCAM and, most recently, HDTV. The development from HDDV to HDTV has been that from specific cameras to the overall cinematographic process. But to find filmmakers as commercially and ideologically opposed as Lars von Trier and George Lucas using the same systems also goes some way to tracing the *convergent* developments at work here. Post-Dogme, von Trier has worked with 35mm film in *Breaking the Waves* (1996), DVCAM on *Dancer in the Dark* (2000) and HDTV on *Dogville* (2003). Justified in terms of technical innovation, Lucas made use of HDCAM equipment for *Star Wars* Episode II and the HDTV process for Episode III. The shift from CAMs to TV also demonstrates the further synergy between film and television. DV is now used regularly in television production. And HDTV, first used in the Spielberg-produced mini-series *Band of Brothers* (2001), has come to be utilized in recent feature films such as Robert Rodriguez's *Once Upon a Time in Mexico* (2003) and *Sin City*, and Michael Mann's *Collateral* (2004). This allows for the speed of television production but also the versatility and clarity of the digital image.

As British director, Mike Figgis, has assessed the situation from an independent perspective:

> Hollywood are terrified. They are afraid, they're absolutely terrified, because if I can prove that I can make a film for, say, £100,000 – a feature film with stars – and the equipment that I will use will go in the boot of my car; that is a terrifying prospect for an industry that's over-invested in hardware . . . And so what Hollywood has now done, which I think is really dumb, is they're pretending that the digital revolution is this thing called High-Definition and Lucassound and Lucas this and Lucas that. What they're really trying to do is divert the onslaught by saying we're really on the same side as you. However, what they're saying is please don't take our big things away from us.[1]

Leading to a new dominance and uniformity to a certain extent, as things currently stand, however, along with analogue video and film, DV and HD more correctly provide for a *range* of options and aesthetics. Consider the use of thirty DV cameras in *Julien Donkey-Boy*, for example, and the clarity of HD in the *Star Wars* prequels. And then consider the use of DV and HD in the moody, ambient night-time aesthetics of *Collateral*.

In the following case studies, I will be focusing on the use of digital video in terms of film form, aesthetics and genre. Mike Figgis's *Timecode* represents a particular experiment in conventional film form, progressing as it does entirely through split-screens. Independent filmmaking criteria remain in terms of low budgets leading to the necessity of experimentation but how do the alternative modes of digital video translate into a genre such as horror? In the second case study, I will explore this question in relation to Marc Evans's *My Little Eye* and Danny Boyle's *28 Days Later*. In the first example, I will be looking primarily at film form and, in the second, DV aesthetics.

Case study 1

TIMECODE (2000)

Mike Figgis's *Timecode* presents us with a linear, split-screen narrative, the principal distinctions being that the story progresses in real time over four screens, our attention drawn to the main characters who inhabit each and ultimately every quarter of the screen through variances in sound. Lev Manovich and Keith Griffiths take leave to question exactly how experimental we should regard the film. 'Although it adopts some of the visual conventions of computer culture,' states Manovich, 'it does not yet deal with the underlying logic of a computer code' (Manovich 2002: 217). And, while valuing its 'playful storytelling and narrative order', Griffiths argues that 'in terms of altering the actual surface or the palette of the film, *Timecode* remains strictly conventional' (Griffiths 2003: 20). As a digitally experimental feature film, however, *Timecode* remains an excellent introduction to the ways in which digital video can be used to subvert conventional aspects of film form and narrative.

First of all, could *Timecode* have been produced as an analogue, 35mm film? As Figgis states, he was particularly inspired by the multi-character, multi-narrative films of Robert Altman. Similar to Altman's *The Player* (1992) and *Short Cuts* (1993) in terms of setting and situations, the principal way in which *Timecode* distinguishes itself from Altman's films is that we can see all of the characters at once through use of the split-screen technique in what Figgis terms a 'four dimensional' multi-narrative film.[2] The first familiarity of the film is that it is set in the film world of Los Angeles. The second familiarity is how the film plays out with regard to genre. As Lev Manovich argues, the problem with the 'real time' technique of DV films such as *Festen* and *Timecode* is that we are often presented with *more* incidents than 'the artificially compressed time of traditional film narrative' (Manovich 2002: 214–15). Multi-generic in terms of mixing comedy, drama, sex and murder, the compression resulting out of both temporal flow and spatial organization within *Timecode* presents us with clichés that are also deliberate. As the banal sex drama of the casting sessions and the pretentious boardroom presentation suggest, both mainstream and arthouse filmmaking are variously taken to task in the film.

Based around a behind-the-scenes story that can also be regarded as metafictional, the ways in which that story is presented to us is where the real experimentation lies. As we have already discussed, one of the main advantages of DV filmmaking is that production and postproduction are brought closer together. In order to think in four dimensions, the musically trained Figgis wrote the narrative of the film on music manuscript, allowing the essential construction and development to be written on four lines of parallel action over a six-page script or 'score'. The actors were then involved in one week of improvisation to flesh out the characters and dialogue. Tightly synchronized in terms of the dance of cameras, fifteen continuous 93-minute takes were performed over the next three weeks, the cast and crew immediately able to watch each version of the film and develop accordingly throughout the overall process. Absent of editing and special effects, postproduction was accomplished almost entirely through sound mixing.

These production elements are only useful insofar as they go on to inform the actual film text. Film producer Alex (Stellan Skarsgard) is having a relationship with actresses Emma (Saffron Burrows) and Rose (Salma Hayek). This would be a conventional love triangle were it not for the fact that Rose is also involved with her agent, Lauren (Jeanne Tripplehorn). Shaped by the form of the film, this love quadrangle plays out across four screens. The opening fifteen minutes of *Timecode* work in terms of a conventional introduction but also allow for formal orientation as each of the main characters is established in a separate screen. Prefaced by the earthquake that affects all of the characters, however, the rest of the film will see the main players intersecting as the initially very formal split-screen structure is given fluidity. The congress of characters starts to play through screen breaks: Emma from the top-right Screen 2 and then Rose from top-left Screen 1 individually meeting up with Alex in bottom-right Screen 4 and bottom-left Screen 3. In accordance with a developing distinction, the top half of the screen shows characters in transit feeding into and out of the main events in the film production world at the bottom half of the screen. The first screen break occurs when Emma arrives at the Red Mullet offices. We see her entering from her own screen, Screen 2, and she simultaneously appears in Screens 2 and 4 as she kisses Alex, which also involves a symbolic split after the join as a reverse shot shows Alex in Screen 2 and Emma in Screen 4. Each has entered into the other's screen worlds and, significantly, Alex is the only character to appear in all four screens. Further, promiscuous, screen breaks occur during the sex scene between Rose and Alex, which takes place in and across Screens 3 and 4. A singular focus in mainstream films, while our attention is drawn to the two lovers, it is also illicit as they make love behind the screen test of a love scene being projected on Screens 1 and 2. In tight frames whose only light and sound are provided by the screen test, such as Lauren listening in on the act, we too are left trying to distinguish the real sex from the film-within-a-film sex. This segment of *Timecode* ends with all four characters alone with their thoughts, Emma and Rose looking in the mirror in Screens 2 and 4, and Lauren and Alex unaware of each other having a cigarette outside the offices in Screens 1 and 3.

As well as subverting traditional film conventions, *Timecode* also makes use of aspects of new media. It does so through both form and content; that is, what we see on screen and what the characters do on screen. In his analysis of what he calls '*DV realism*', Lev Manovich regards the immediacy of spatially aware real time DV films as being the result of tapping into today's '*reality media*', principally reality television and webcams. Manovich regards *Timecode* as utilizing formal aspects of modern telecommunications but, again, built upon relatively traditional narrative bases (Manovich 2002: 215–16). Using new technologies of seeing and surveillance is not the sole preserve of DV realism, having been used in films and television series like *The Matrix* and *24*, and in non-narrative video and performance art. Essentially, however, *Timecode* can be located outside such high-tech plotting and the denial of narrative in what is, after all, a character-driven film. If this is part of its so-called conventional narrative, the point is that much more reliance on new technologies would marginalize the film's characters, who remain our principal focus throughout.

Beginning with the split-screen technique, *Timecode* echoes the windowed properties of contemporary media, whether the internet, DVDs or even multiplayer videogames (see also Hanson 2003: 70–1; Verevis 2005). The four quarters also have the effect of chopping this piece of cinema down to television or computer monitor size, a reduction of potential scale in favour of intimacy and a surveillance-style invasion of privacy. Surveillance and voyeurism are principally conveyed through the roving cameras. Where one camera is usually enough for the innate voyeurism of film viewers, here the four cameras cover events from all distances and angles, often when hiding behind objects (the literal result of each cameraman not wanting to be exposed by the other cameras). This verité style, which also involves out-of-focus shots and imperfect framing, is followed through to the sound mixing in terms of tuning in and out of snatches of conversation.

If most of this relates to what the film viewer sees, the characters within *Timecode* are also connected by various technologies. The security guard would be the closest to providing an omniscient perspective if he weren't so distracted from his CCTV monitors when peddling drugs. All of the main characters are connected by the film-production world they inhabit and it's significant that technology is only explicitly foregrounded here when Anna (Mia Maestro) presents Red Mullet with a discourse on digital film complete with DJ and a live soundtrack demonstration. Sound technologies play a part in the developing narrative of the film in terms of surveillance, connection and disconnection, principally Lauren's bugging of Rose and assorted arrangements made on mobile phones. *Timecode* ends with a film camera and the mobile phone. Avant-garde director Anna films the death of mainstream producer Alex, her ambition for pure vérité given its ultimate demonstration. And the final scene of the film involves mobile phone calls across all four screens: Rose phoning Lauren, who doesn't answer the call; and the dying Alex phoning Emma, his final moments caught on film and his last words transmitted over a phone line inaudible to the film viewer. Overall, then, *Timecode* focuses on two developments: the recent potential for digital filmmaking and the ways in which film will have to adapt to new media technologies. It concludes with ambivalence, the cold substantial art of film and the final connection made on something as seemingly insignificant as a mobile phone.

<hr />

Case study 2

MY LITTLE EYE (2002) AND *28 DAYS LATER* (2002)

From *The Night of the Living Dead* (1968) and *The Texas Chainsaw Massacre* (1974) to *The Blair Witch Project* and current retrograde slasher films, the horror genre progresses by continually going back to basics. As Matt Hanson states: 'Cinematic horror has always been at its eeriest and its most convincing when stripped down. The genre is at its best flayed of all pretensions or extraneous details – any hint, in fact, that what is happening has any root in artifice' (Hanson 2003: 13). Although it is too soon – or possibly too late – to talk about a definitive wave of DV horror films, a new post-*Blair Witch* aesthetic has developed through various uses of film and video. Hence, for example, *Wendigo* (2001), which makes use of 16mm, and *Session 9* (2001), which was one of the first films to use HDDV (see Aloi 2005). The same 'authenticity' can be found in *The Descent* (2005), which makes use of film, video and camcorder formats, and *Wolf Creek* (2005), which uses HDTV. The purest examples of DV horror are Marc Evans's *My Little Eye* and Danny Boyle's *28 Days Later*. Enabling a back-to-basics approach to some of the most effective horror conventions, digital video provided these films with a much more versatile aesthetic and also allowed for a formal rearrangement of the more expected material of the genre.

My Little Eye combines the two main outlets of today's 'reality' media: reality television and the internet. In the first instance, the film is grounded in many of the recent conventions of *Big Brother*-style television shows: audition tapes; a group of participants isolated in a house for a determinate period and ultimate prize; all-seeing cameras; and the occasional delivery or surprise designed to breathe life or breed more contempt into contestants so that viewers will keep watching. Beyond this, however, the live internet format chosen for the film makes it much more speculative in that current webcasts are not as advanced or organized. In a sense, therefore, the film takes us into what could have been had reality television not proven a more acceptable version of the sort of voyeuristic material privately available on the internet. But this, of course, is exaggerated as appropriate to make it into a horror film.

My Little Eye creates much of its atmosphere through the combination of sound and images. Opening with a pixellated glaze and the sound of a modem, the camera pulls back to reveal a computer screen. The first of many associations between passive film voyeur and interactive computer user, the anonymous user clicks on a 'Wanted!' pop-up which results in the following text:

5 contestants for REALITY WEBCAST
Spend 6 months in a house for $1 MILLION
If anyone leaves, everyone loses!
R U the perfect housemate?
CLICK TO ENTER

Following on from the actual film title, we are then introduced to the main characters via their audition tapes. Having themselves clicked to enter, these participants soon find themselves unwitting victims of a 'snuff' webcast through which subscribers bet on their fluctuating odds of survival.

Rarely breaking the point-of-view perspective of the adopted webcast format, *My Little Eye* works in simultaneously 'framing' the characters and directing what we see on screen. Horror cinema has always been about positioning, the viewer made to identify with the victim or even the killer. Here, the webcast format allows for a further level, the director Evans in complete control but on a parallel with 'The Company' in the film. In the opening sequence, we are provided with a four-quartered split-screen montage of the participants' arrival and first months in the house. Resembling *Timecode* in terms of spatial organization, this initial technique allows for the compression of time similar to the ways in which reality television gives us edited highlights or the internet subscriber might look through archive material. The first uneventful weeks in the house bypassed and, moving on to full screen, what would otherwise be presented as five stock teenagers chatting their way through exposition becomes a way of familiarizing the viewer to the film's defamiliarizing form. Shot mostly from the top corners of the room and progressing through quick snatches and occasional zooms, we are effectively seeing the action of the film through the myriad surveillance cameras that pervade the house. All movement of the cameras is accompanied by electronic clicks and whirrs, and the film takes on further distance and involvement when the participants are shot via two-way mirrors, for example, or from outside-in. Privacy is obviously not an option in the house and this is made clear when the participants go to bed in the subsequent scene. Feeling safer in the darkness, the participants are nevertheless illuminated by the green haze of infra-red cameras and monitored by further sound devices. Talking about the males in the house, for example, the female characters whisper. But similar to the way in which the cameras focus in to avoid blurred images, the sound devices work in clarifying muffled sounds. Throughout the film, the more the assumed privacy, the more the probing intensity of techniques.

As producer Jon Finn states, *My Little Eye* is a 'low-tech' film that uses camera equipment bought from high street retailers.[3] Compare this with two other internet-themed horror films from 2002 – *FearDotCom* and *Halloween: Resurrection* – and the overall digital effects of the film become much more pronounced. One of the subsequent values of using consumer-grade digital cameras was exactly the ability to explore surveillance, which becomes most illicit and paradoxically evident when small cameras are attached to pens, torches, a joypad and a shower nozzle. Talking further about the challenges and advantages of shooting *My Little Eye* in this way, Finn claims it a piece of 'anti-filmmaking'. Which is to say that the film has to follow the webcast format throughout and this also determines the ways in which it works as a horror film. Viewing the majority of the action through locked-on cameras means that using familiar horror film conventions such as point-of-view shots or overtly skewed angles is not a viable option. Working within this small screen format, however, has its advantages with regard to horror. Exaggerating the characteristic complicity of horror film viewers and further restricting the participants' movement and actions, the format shapes both the participants' unease and ours. It is in this respect that we can see the variety of camera shots as *extending* horror film conventions. As Marc Evans states, the main difference is that instead of 'anticipating' the action, the cameras are 'behind' the action. Referring to specific moments where the cameras take advantage of how exposed the participants are by locking on to the backs of their heads and necks, this also refers to the way in which the film viewer follows the action. In effect we find ourselves positioned *between* The Company and the participants, essentially powerless but with a wider perspective than the participants. The final revelation might still come as something of a surprise but at this point we're fully complicit in the game.

Freed from the formal requirements of *My Little Eye*, Danny Boyle's *28 Days Later* allows us to look much more at DV aesthetics. A post-apocalyptic zombie film that works through urban desolation, it makes stark use of contrasts, principally day and night on a visual level, and peace and rage on an allied aural level. Following the necessary horror mechanics to a certain extent (the Infected only come out at night), these contrasts are first accentuated and then blurred by the use of digital video. Following on from the dark, claustrophobic laboratory and the hit-and-run pace of the opening sequence, the film immediately progresses to a barren London hospital where Jim (Cillian Murphy) wakes up bathed in glaring light. As Jim becomes accustomed to the light, it takes on more of a dreamlike hue which is continued as he leaves the hospital and walks out into a deserted London. Throughout the London sequence as a whole, the DV cameras work through emphasis and de-emphasis. The camera angles both frame and cut across the straight lines of the buildings, advertising hoardings and familiar landmarks. This is at once a city laid bare – an architectural grid without the usual organic mass of people – and a city in an unfamiliar situation where the lack of people is exactly the thing that allows our attention to be drawn to the skewed geometry of the buildings. Long shots and close-ups follow Jim's isolation through what becomes a montage sequence and the dreamlike hue takes on more of an environmental blur. As the sun beats down on silver structures through the rising haze, it's a hot day but it also looks like post-nuclear.

For Danny Boyle and Anthony Dod Mantle, cinematographer of *Festen*, *Julien Donkey-Boy* and *Dogville*, this London sequence proved to be the biggest advantage with regard to using digital video. Prepared beforehand with digital photographs of the city and given one morning to shoot the sequence, the use of several cameras allowed for unlimited footage from numerous angles to be edited together in postproduction. Speaking further of the use of DV in *28 Days Later*, Boyle highlights two other benefits:

> We wanted it to feel different in texture from normal film. Because it's an apocalypse, you can use a different hue, because nobody knows what things will look like if everybody's killed or there are no cars. So . . . we would tickle the color of the film occasionally to create a slightly strange universe. Against that, I wanted this enormous energy from those who are infected, which I was going to get through this particular menu on the camera, which allows you to alter the frame rate; things appear to be speeded up but actually it's real time. So you kind of snatch at fast images, like falling rain or a man running, snatching at them in a slightly unreliable way. The idea is that you can't quite trust your usual sense of judgment about perception, depth and distance when dealing with the infected. (Quoted in Hunter 2003: 2)

Boyle has also justified his choice of digital video in terms of the predominantly urban nature of the film. Speaking in particular about the British context, we are indeed very used to seeing the pervasive coverage and grainy aesthetic of CCTV cameras. When applied to the film this can be taken very literally in that, if there were an apocalypse of some sort, then there wouldn't be a film crew to record the after-events.[4]

Far from presenting us with omniscient camera shots surveying empty streets, the action scenes in *28 Days Later* are conveyed through abrupt editing and often presented in terms of sudden environmental effects. Hence, when Selena (Naomie Harris) and Mark (Noah Huntley) rescue Jim by petrol-bombing a service station, the impact is also that of light exploding into dark. Conversely, smashing through windows or scrambling over barriers, when the Infected attack it is presented in terms of the dark trying to break through receding sources of light. From the sunny South to the rainy North, the climax to the film takes place in a baroque country house. And, moving on from the previous urban effects, the digital aesthetics now work in conveying a gothic atmosphere. If we were to isolate the action elements of the film from the atmospheric, it would principally be a matter of looking at the moments of physical violence. From individual attacks to the final onslaught, the staccato movement of the Infected is the most noticeable action effect within the film. Filmed with the camera shooting at variances between 24 and 16,000 frames per second, the Infected run and attack through blinks of the eye. It is only when the same technique is applied to environmental effects, however, that the action sequences represent a full onslaught as it is illuminated by speckled flashes of gunfire, lightning and searchlights. Rain takes on the appearance of liquid metal and, more so than ever, the cameras can barely isolate the Infected as they smash through doors and windows. And Jim is himself filmed in the same manner as he moves between the soldiers and zombies, ultimately leading us to question whose side he is on and whether he too has become Infected.

The digital composition and aesthetics of *28 Days Later* take us into a world divorced from our own, and to the extent that any flashes of the familiar appear in stark relief. There is something too perfect about the impressionistic and almost hyperreal blue skies and green fields on the road from London to Manchester, for example. But it is entirely fitting that moments of comfort in the film use different, familiar, film stocks. When Jim visits his family home in the suburbs, for example, his thoughts become a Super 8 flashback. And the fact that the final scene of the film is shot using 35mm film is also significant in that we, the audience, are very familiar with that look. Framed by a jet scouring the countryside, the three survivors are rescued and we too are released, re-conditioned, back into widescreen clarity and out of the film.

3 Digital special effects

At its widest, to move from digital video to digital special effects is to progress from independent film to blockbusters and from the immediate on-location use of digital cameras to the machinery of postproduction. Where arguments surrounding independent versus mainstream production provide us with one way in to exploring digital film, the use of digital special effects can be regarded as a debate *within* mainstream and blockbusting cinema. This is based on the distinction between 'visible' and 'invisible' effects. Where invisible effects work is used in relation to backgrounds and detail, visible effects are designed to be noticed. Giving life to amazing sights and finding their main drive in action sequences, these are the effects that are meant to be special and spectacular (see, for example, Buckland 1999; Mak 2003).

In this chapter, I will be looking at digital special effects in terms of contradiction and synthesis. Where special effects have always been regarded in terms of excess or integration, digital special effects bring us round to the essentials of computerization as applied to film – principally the ways in which effects essentially generated within computers have successfully or otherwise been integrated into the familiar palette and parameters of the photographic. I will begin with the ways in which digital special effects have been regarded in terms of ambivalence. This will be highlighted in terms of science fiction cinema and the 'spectacle versus narrative' argument as applied to contemporary Hollywood blockbusters. Simultaneously more successful and spectacular, I will then look at the development of digital special effects in terms of integration and synthesis. Here, I will be exploring the use of digital special effects in a range of film genres and extending to questions of realism in CG animation. For my chosen case studies I will be looking at the spectacle versus narrative debate as applied to *Star Wars Episode II: Attack of the Clones*, and notions of spectacle and realism in relation to the digital character of Gollum in *The Lord of the Rings: The Two Towers*.

From contradiction to integration

Early work on digital special effects comes to us in terms of 'disruption', 'contradiction' and 'ambivalence'. Special effects have been said to disrupt the normal course of film viewing in terms of: (i) narrative, (ii) form, and (iii) aesthetics. Although one tendency is to place all of these properties under the aegis of film narrative, it is useful to distinguish narrative in terms of structure, conventionally the ways in which we are given a story to follow over the course of two hours or so and the ways in which that story is presented to us in terms of plot and chronology. Narrowed down to such structural and more specifically **narratological** properties, the spectacle versus narrative argument goes as follows. Whereas narrative is classically said to give drive, coherence and meaning to a film, spectacle has traditionally been regarded in terms of self-contained moments of visual excess. Seen in these terms, spectacle in effect short-circuits narrative, almost putting the film on hold while we're pulled into some other dimension where action and effects take over from more 'natural' storytelling properties such as character development and dramatic revelations. This isn't new. Criticism of action, spectacle and special effects is very often a criticism of genre and the same has been said of comedy slapstick sequences and show-stopping musical numbers. The current state of play, however, has been traced back to the beginnings of New Hollywood Cinema in the late 1960s. While the experimental disruption of narrative in films such as *Bonnie and Clyde* (1967) and *The Graduate* (1967) has been regarded as a bona fide challenge – the beginnings of more fragmented 'post-classical' narratives – from *Jaws* (1975) and *Star Wars* (1977) onwards, the argument is that narrative has simply been sidelined in contemporary blockbusters and that, depending on how cardboard the characters or perfunctory the plot, audiences just sit back and wait for the next big action sequence (see, for example, Lewis 1998; Neale and Smith 1998; King 2002).

The argument that blockbusters favour spectacle over narrative is, first, an observation but also something of an innate value judgement, familiar from film review criticism, that special effects are artificially constructed rather than artfully deployed. Readings that value narrative over spectacle, however, can be countered in several ways, not least the refusal to recognize that what distinguishes cinema most of all, from literature and the fine arts for example, is that it is a sight-and-sound medium. The tendency to value narrative and only narrative can be reductive and unforgiving. The narratological approach, in many ways carried over from literary studies, often reduces films to one dimension, that of a singularly *temporal* cohesion and progression. Stripped down to a line on a graph – neat cohesion down one side and tidy progression along the other – the meaning and significance of narrative principally derive from an over-appreciation of classical Hollywood cinema. As Geoff King argues:

> If some of the products of the studio era do seem unified, balanced, coherent and 'well-made', it is doubtful that this was ever an overriding imperative. Profitability has usually been more important than unity or homogeneity. The desire to appeal to a mass market is likely to produce a degree of built-in *in*coherence and conflicting demands. Spectacle is often just as much a core aspect of Hollywood cinema as coherent narrative and should not necessarily be seen as a disruptive intrusion from some place outside. The coherence, or drive towards coherence, often ascribed to classical Hollywood films can be a product of a particular kind of critical reading rather than a quality of the text itself. (King 2000: 3–4).

Film form and aesthetics

Although providing a way in with regard to film structure, the narrative approach gains more depth when combined with consideration of film form and aesthetic. The formal and aesthetic arguments refer to those moments when we might think 'that's obviously a special effect' or 'what an amazing special effect'. Our mind is taken off the supposed realism or believability of what we are presented with and the illusion is shattered. Looking at aspects of form allows us to look much more specifically at film technique, the ways in which special effects sequences may or may not fit into the design and shape of the film as a whole. Similarly, the aesthetic extends to the perceptual properties of film viewing, principally whether we can see the 'join' or not. The problem with the strictly narrative approach is that any action sequence can be regarded as an interruption. Consideration of form brings us much closer to the ways in which particular aspects of special effects work are combined with existing film techniques: that is, the overall fit and feel of effects sequences. And the aesthetic approach is particularly relevant to digital special effects. Should the effects appear too flat or fake then our willing suspension of disbelief is put on hold while we ruminate upon obvious or unsatisfactory effects work. Even the opposite is true, in that the more successful the effect the more we will be asking 'how did they do that?'

The first genre to receive attention with regard to digital special effects was science fiction. With its fetish for advanced technologies and characteristic attempts to represent the 'other' and the 'unknown', science fiction cinema relies on giving shape and substance to otherwise alien, futuristic concepts. But looking at the ways in which science fiction cinema also fails to do that has been the first step towards understanding the contradictions inherent in special effects. As Brooks Landon and Vivian Sobchack argue, there is first of all a contradiction between the 'show' and 'tell' of science fiction films. In the main, science fiction cinema presents us with a critique of science and technology. This is where it gets its drama from, understood in traditional storytelling terms of conflict and resolution. The problem with special effects, therefore, is that the 'show' often overrides the 'tell', which is to say that the critique is lost to the technical prowess that we see before us in often supercharged special effects sequences. Landon terms this the 'aesthetics of ambivalence', which occurs when 'the production technology of a film is so seductive that the technological accomplishment of the film sends a quite different message than does its narrative' (Landon 1992: xxv). Developing this point with less favourable ambivalence than Landon, Sobchack goes on to look at special effects in science fiction cinema of the 1970s and 1980s. Whereas science fiction films of the 1960s and early 1970s tended to be cold and clinical, the more special effects-driven space operas from the late 1970s and the 1980s retreated into a glossy, kinetic, technological aesthetic where the main emphasis can only be described as fun. As Sobchack herself plays with the language of contradiction:

> In the genre's earlier period, special effects generally functioned to symbolize the 'rational coolness' (and fearsome 'coldness') associated with high technology and scientific objectivity, and were 'authenticated' and made credible by the genre's 'documentary' visual attitude. In

contrast, today's special effects generally function to symbolize the 'irrational warmth' of intense (and usually positive) emotions, and their credibility is not the issue. The genre has transformed its 'objective' representation of a 'high' technology into the 'subjective' symbolization of a technologized 'high' (Sobchack 1993: 282).

Computer-generated imaging

Landon and Sobchack's work is transitional in several respects. Bringing attention round to the very subject of special effects, the films that they look at also take us from the previous effects revolution instigated by *Star Wars* – a dynamic combination of motion control, models and matte shots – into embryonic use of computer graphics and animation in films such as: *Futureworld* (1976), *Star Trek II: The Wrath of Khan* (1982), *Tron* (1982), *War Games* (1983) and *The Last Starfighter* (1984) (see also Bukatman 1993). The sole preserve of computer display sequences, space battles and early flights into cyberspace, in the 1990s computer graphics gave way to the much more consolidated and diverse use of computer-generated imaging. This allows images to be placed within the context of the normal and the familiar, in terms of both physical locations and environments, and the three-dimensional space of film itself. CGI was first used in 'obvious' effects sequences in *Young Sherlock Holmes* (1985), *Star Trek IV: The Voyage Home* (1986) and *Willow* (1988) (see Darley 2000; Griffiths 2003). But it was James Cameron's *The Abyss* (1989) that first demonstrated the photorealistic potential of CGI. An underwater science fiction film, the liquid morphing alien that appears for two minutes was a suitable mix of the familiar and the unfamiliar; the process involving the computer generation of water, within physical surroundings, in shape-shifting alien form. Both solid and unstable, morphing can be seen as the ideal introduction for CGI and was successfully followed through to Cameron's *Terminator 2: Judgment Day* (1991). Given its physical grounding in Robert Patrick's performance, the liquid metal T1000 cyborg could be seen in pure, intermediate and fully humanoid form; the strong, sinewy and globular pitted against muscle man, Arnold Schwarzenegger. And this is very much the way in which CGI first took hold: a wonder to behold grounded in physical space and increasingly involved action sequences. Steven Spielberg's *Jurassic Park* (1993) can be regarded in very much the same way. Here, the

CG dinosaurs were given solidity, texture and weight in numerous ways. Combined with animatronic dinosaurs – a foot in the mud here, descending jaws in the torchlight there – the T-Rex attack, in particular, is an excellent, if technically very careful, example of the early integration of CGI. *Terminator 2* and *Jurassic Park* proved the technical success and commercial viability of CGI and can now be regarded as canonical classics of the form (see Ndalianis 2000; Manovich 2001; Allen 2002).

As Michelle Pierson argues, 1989 to 1995 were the 'wonder years' of CGI, when audiences were literally invited to (i) watch a film because of its novel special effects and (ii) gaze in awe at them. Pierson deconstructs this 'self-consciousness' in two ways, the films offering definite lo-and-behold sequences on the one hand but in an early aesthetic necessarily caught between 'photographic realism' and 'a synthetic hyperrealism' (Pierson 1999: 172; see also Pierson 2002: 93–136). Which is to say that Hollywood was also able to benefit from the relative limitations of CGI, that what cinema audiences were being presented with was, indeed, something new and distinct. This self-consciousness was also reflected through the narrative of the films, the most notable examples from this period essentially being *about* bringing forms to life. Hence the state-of-the-art T1000 squaring up to the relatively industrial T800 in *Terminator 2* and the resurrection of dinosaurs in *Jurassic Park*. This narrative element is also what partly allowed CGI to spread to other genres throughout the 1990s: automatically connecting with the anthropomorphic spirit of animation in *Toy Story* (1995), *Antz* (1997) and *A Bug's Life* (1997); the re-presentation of history in *Titanic* (1997); and fantasy adventure films such as *Jumanji* (1995) and *The Mummy* (1999).

From integration to synthesis

Since the late 1990s, computer-generated imaging has become the cinematic standard in special effects. Indeed, we are at the point now where the decidedly industrial acronym of CGI hardly suffices when considering the numerous uses to which digital special effects have been put. While science fiction still provides us with the most obvious examples, digital effects have come to be used in a range of genres old and new (see Keane 2006). The principal genres I would highlight in this respect are:

- Disaster movies: from the late 1990s cycle of films such as *Twister* (1996), *Titanic* and *Armageddon* (1998) through to *The Day After Tomorrow* (2004) and *Poseidon* (2006).
- Sword-and-sandal epics: such as *Gladiator* (2000) and *Troy* (2004).
- Historical epics: such as *Master and Commander: The Far Side of the World* (2003) and *The Last Crusade* (2005).
- Fantasy films: from *Lord of the Rings* (2001–3) and *Harry Potter* (2001–) to *The Chronicles of Narnia* (2005–).
- Superhero movies: from *X-Men* (2000) to *Spider-Man 3* (2007).

Integration

As Sean Cubitt (2002 and 2004) argues, digital effects have become successful because they have come to replicate and in many cases gone on to replace prior special-effects techniques. Driven by the political economy of more spectacle at reasonable cost, Cubitt starts by isolating model work and art direction. From the original stop-motion King Kong to the combined animatronics and CGI of *Jurassic Park*, we see the same thing – basically monsters – but in new and more advanced ways. Similarly with regard to rear projection, painted backdrops and traditional matte work. These practices have given way to widespread use of blue- and green-screen processes that provide for three-dimensional backdrops and environments, and more recently, **virtual sets**. More often than not, digital effects have worked through the simulation and improvement of existing film techniques. This is particularly evident in **motion capture** and **motion control**. As Michael Allen argues, however, these technical considerations are only important insofar as they fit into the existing narrative, formal and aesthetic dimensions of the resulting film texts. In his excellent close analysis of *The Abyss*, *Jurassic Park* and *Godzilla* (1998), he deconstructs the films in terms of: shot length; the framing of live and digital elements; more dynamic camera movement in both analogue and motion control; the increased blurring of the live and the virtual; and the placing and timing of CG sequences. As Allen concludes:

> In using and manipulating the formal parameters of mainstream film-making in this way, CGI sequences construct themselves as simultaneously ordinary *and* extraordinary, as photo-realistic elements of

transparent film-making and as non-real, spectacular images designed to be noticed, to be separated from the flow of the rest of the film's images, and appreciated for their non-photographic visual qualities. The tension between these two states, between these two kinds of film form, has come to typify the experience of watching any film with a significant degree of CGI in it. (Allen 2002: 117–18)

In a more confident development of the self-consciousness identified by Michelle Pierson, this tension now works in retaining the special effect of digital effects. This can now be regarded on three levels: the ability to combine the digital with the photographic; the ability to simulate pre-existing film techniques; and the ability to remain distinctly spectacular.

Animation

Both Cubitt and Allen look at the material integration of digital effects: that is, within the context of live-action feature films. The most complete synthesis, however, takes place within animated feature films. Where integration implies the successful combination of two previously separate elements, synthesis represents a much more fluid proposition. The history of computer-generated animation is almost as well documented as the initial relationship between CGI and science fiction cinema. Whereas that was first broached in terms of an aesthetics of ambivalence, however, CGA is inherently simulationist. Which is to say that it takes place within a much more transparently synthetic genre. Eschewing the spectacle versus narrative argument as applied to CGI and live-action feature films, therefore, much of the work on CGA has related to varying levels of *realism*. Or, to put it another way, how can one distinguish special effects sequences in animated films that are, essentially, entirely composed of special effects? The fact that we can talk about *levels* of realism, however, demonstrates that animation is not without its own problems of assimilation. The main developments can be outlined as follows:

(i)   the ways in which CGA compares and contrasts with traditional animation;
(ii) the ways in which CGA has resulted in its own aesthetic; and
(iii) the ways in which CGA compares and contrasts with live-action feature films that make extensive use of digital effects and aesthetics.

As Paul Wells argues, animation has always been caught between 'mimesis' and 'abstraction' (Wells 2001: 4–5). If one tendency of the dominant Disney style was to provide for a middle ground between anthropomorphic realism and fairy-tale fantasy, CGA has essentially brought us back to initial distinctions. These are most apparent in the first fully computer-animated feature film, *Toy Story*. As Wells states:

> The success of *Toy Story* created a 'professional' aesthetic for CGI which, while not creating an 'orthodoxy' for the form nevertheless confirmed the potential of the medium by fully exploiting its distinctive credentials. The toys exemplified the 'plasticity' and 'gloss' of geometric forms created in CGI, while the movement through the domestic space properly revealed the sense of depth and space in virtual three-dimensionality. (Wells 2001: 13)

Where CGA was first used in isolated sequences in Disney's *Beauty and the Beast* (1992) and *The Lion King* (1994), full CGA films work through a much more pervasive remediation. In what Andrew Darley terms 'secondary' or 'second-order' realism, *Toy Story* represents a 'synthetic blending or *fusing* via the computer of certain prior image forms'. Disney-style animation, live-action cinema and three-dimensional puppet animation provide 'a partial *model* for the programmers to aim for in the search for heightened illusionism'. As Darley goes on to argue, however, this search for realism can be overpowering, an overriding technical mission for the animators and something of a niggling fascination for audiences (Darley 2000: 82–8). But the particular trick of remediation is that it works backwards and forwards, providing an initial model for animators and an initial familiarity for audiences. Technical demands accomplished and audiences more exposed to this new aesthetic, the films are then able to relax back into story and characterization (see Bolter and Grusin 1999: 147–50; Barker 2000; Sarafian 2003).

Less geometric in its forms and more fluid and cinematic in terms of action and environments, CGA has now become a definite aesthetic for a renewed genre. With regard to comparisons with contemporary live-action cinema, however, the distinction still remains. Becoming less *animated* films and more animated *films*, they still characteristically fall short of full photorealism. This is particularly manifest in the recent Pixar production, *The Incredibles* (2004). Garnering more critical praise than its commercially more successful rival, DreamWorks' *Shrek 2* (2004), *The Incredibles* has been valued in terms of its more 'adult' story and can principally be distinguished by the fact that it focuses exclusively on human characters. Centred around a middle-aged former superhero and his family, it is a drama and an action film, the former relying on convincing performances and the latter all the kinetic appeal of a superhero movie. Like many CGA films, *The Incredibles* gains much of its weight and naturalism from sound, music and the voice talents of its principal actors. The most notable CGA films such as *Toy Story*, *A Bug's Life*, *Monsters Inc.* (2001) and *Finding Nemo* (2003) are very much in keeping with the anthropomorphic spirit of animation. *Shrek* (2001) and *Shrek 2* may well have featured more human characters but they are still caricatures in keeping with the films' anti-fairy tale quality. The human characters in *The Incredibles* are also superhuman but, combined with the deliberate comic book feel of the film, they can be said to have progressed from 'plastic' to 'elastic', the 'rubber' look of previous human characters in CGA given more refined, expressive capabilities and these readily translating into the film's action sequences. Given superpowers that simultaneously define and result from their characters, the family comes together to use their dormant powers of strength, speed, invisibility and elasticity. The film does remain stylized but comes to represent a relatively seamless fusing of narrative and spectacle. Much more than live-action blockbusters, there is little arguing about the 'join' or the 'fit' as *The Incredibles* puts its animated characters into action.

In the first case study, I will look at the spectacle versus narrative argument as applied to *Attack of the Clones*, a live-action feature film that makes extensive and potentially overriding use of digital aesthetics and effects. In the second case study, I will be looking at spectacle and realism in relation to the digitally 'animated' character of Gollum in *The Two Towers*. Both of these films can be used to address the range of factors outlined above, from possible contradiction to potential integration and synthesis.

Case study 3

STAR WARS EPISODE II: ATTACK OF THE CLONES (2002)

One retrospect provided by the *Star Wars* prequels, Episodes I to III, is that Episodes IV to VI are now commonly referred to as 'the originals'. This is but one sign that getting to the heart of the prequels, as narrative 'continuations' of the saga, was always going to feature a great deal of prospect and retrospect. One of the first invitations in looking at the *Star Wars* prequels in terms of narrative and spectacle, therefore, is to do so in relation to continuity and differences with the original trilogy. Defined as prequels, as predetermined texts whose ending is already known, the narrative draw remains but much less in terms of *what* as *how*. And that realization exists on two levels: the organization of the story and how it is represented visually in terms of design and spectacle.

The 'serial' and 'saga' structure of the *Star Wars* films has been much discussed (see, for example, Keane 2000). Beginning with the famous opening scroll, progressing through cliffhanging moments, and ending with varying degrees of resolution and continuation, each episode of the saga plays its part. The first film in each of the trilogies effectively sets the scene; the second acts as a bridge; and the final film provides us with the conclusion. Seen in these terms, *A New Hope* (1997) and *The Phantom Menace* (1999) remain the most singular in purpose and progression. The main intergalactic conflict is established, those events lead to Tatooine where the central protagonist of each trilogy – Luke Skywalker and father-to-be, Anakin – is introduced, and they are led away by Jedi Knights to take part in the wider scheme of the films. With no guarantee of a future and only retrospectively subtitled 'Episode IV', *A New Hope* remains the most focused of all the *Star Wars* films, its narrative being mainly devoted to rescuing Princess Leia and destroying the Death Star. The challenge, but also the burden, for *The Phantom Menace* was not only to provide the foundations for the prequels but, ultimately, all six films.

As Geoff King and Tanya Krzywinska argue, *The Phantom Menace* 'retains a strong commitment to the narrative dimension' (King and Krzywinska 2000: 103). While the film might not work so well on the uninitiated and any narrative gaps rely too much on the promise that they will go on to be filled in by the subsequent episodes, King and Krzywinska provide us with a textbook narrative reading of the film. Which is to say that, wishing to counter perceptions relating to spectacle over narrative, *The Phantom Menace* does, after all, tell a story. On the level of design, for example, while the exotic planetary locations provide us with a form of spectacle, they also contribute to familiar themes of the saga, characteristically nature and technology, the native and the imperial. With particular regard to action, King and Krzywinska focus on the film's main set-piece, the ten-minute pod race sequence. Again, that this sequence provides us with spectacle is undeniable but it also has its part to play in the narrative of the film and the saga as a whole (King and Krzywinska 2000: 99–110).

Michelle Pierson, however, argues that the narrative dimension of *The Phantom Menace* simply isn't strong enough to draw attention away from the film's visual qualities and those qualities themselves merely add to the wan narrative. In Pierson's account, the prequel nature of the film is a weakness, the ends already known and hence becoming solely a matter of plot mechanics. The temporal draw removed, George Lucas can only fall back on spatial causality in order to give the illusion of progress. Although evident in the original *Star Wars* trilogy, the seemingly faster crosscutting is compounded by the digital nature of these new worlds and the overall digital effect of the film. Giving more depth, as it were, to complaints surrounding the flat, artificial nature of the digital image, Pierson terms this the 'aesthetics of scarcity', that most of the designs in *The Phantom Menace*, however superficially different, are rendered the same. In contrast to King and Krzywinska, therefore, Pierson's argument is that whether forest or metropolis, Jar-Jar Binks or battle droid, so much of this film is digitally animated that it all looks like a simulation:

> In spite of their meticulously layered detail and carefully thought out design, the film's synthetic sequences all have the same simulationist aesthetic horizon. And it is the unwavering commitment to staying within the aesthetic parameters established by this horizon that gives these sequences their unrelieved sameness. If an effect is only special in relation to something else – something that it isn't – how do viewers decide what is a special effect in this context? Does the scope for the kind of transmutation of the visual field that might make an effect special even exist once a film begins to be made over in the mode of an animated feature? (Pierson 2002: 152–3)

Like *The Empire Strikes Back* (1980), the second entry in the original *Star Wars* trilogy, *Attack of the Clones* is all middle. Although starting ten years on from the events in *The Phantom Menace*, it benefits from the backlog of information provided by Episode I and leads much more directly to the events in Episode III. Darker in tone and wider in scope, Episode II is also much more complex in terms of its narrative structure. The film provides us with a wide array of characters and races, a secessionist leader whose motives only gradually become clear, nods backwards and forwards to the other *Star Wars* films, and in the end must present us with a definite progression of the overall story. It is a measure of the densely plotted action and deceptions, in fact, that where *The Empire Strikes Back* is much clearer in its downward turn – the Empire quite simply striking back – *Attack of the Clones* belies its pulp title by having its presumed menace of clones fight *with* the Jedi at the end of the film. Conjoined with consideration of spectacle, therefore, do the visual and kinetic elements of the film help in conveying the potential information overload of the story or simply add to that overload?

Beginning first with spatial organization, *Attack of the Clones* provides us with more worlds than the three planets that help to structure the action in *The Phantom Menace*. Beginning in the capital of the Republic, Coruscant, Episode II then splits off into two stories, the love story and the detective story. In the love story, Anakin (Hayden Christensen) and Amidala (Natalie Portman) return to their home planets. The main courtship takes place in the fertile landscapes of Naboo and tragedy occurs in the barren wasteland of Tatooine. In the detective story, Obi-Wan Kenobi (Ewan McGregor) follows the clone mystery through to the water planet of Kamino and the rock planet of Geonosis where he is taken captive. Anakin and Amidala arrive to rescue him, only themselves to be captured. The final rescue does arrive, however, with the arrival of Jedi Knights from Coruscant and the Clone Army commandeered from Kamino.

If these environments provide us with a backdrop of spectacular locations and help orientate us to the action, the spectacle versus narrative argument has more commonly been related to the ways in action set-pieces either detract from or can be said to contribute to the ongoing narrative of a given film. This refers to spectacle as impact, a much more material aspect than matters of design where the main impact is said to be upon narrative structure. Geoff King provides an appropriate way in to illustrating the impact of major action sequences on the characteristic narrative structure of contemporary blockbusters – a graph. Although there is much more to the enquiry, such a straight-line analysis of moments of spectacle plays structuralist analyses of narrative at their own game, and does provide a way in to understanding the impact of spectacular set-pieces on classical narrative properties such as causality, coherence and flow (King 2002: 185–93). The timing and duration of action moments and sequences in *Attack of the Clones* are as follows:

(i)   3 mins   Assassination attempt on Amidala.

(ii)   13–23 mins   Speeder chase: Obi-Wan and Anakin pursue bounty hunter after second assassination attempt.

(iii) 58–67 mins   One-on-one fight between Obi-Wan and bounty hunter Jango Fett, followed by pursuit in asteroid belt.

(iv) 72–77 mins   Anakin attempts to rescue his mother; mother dies; Anakin slaughters Tusken Raiders.

(v)   83 mins   Obi-Wan captured on Geonosis.

(vi) 93–98 mins   Droid factory: Anakin and Amidala captured.

(vii) 101–126 mins Climax: Obi-Wan, Anakin and Amidala defeat monsters in Geonosian Arena; arrival of secessionist droids and Jedi Knights; rescue of remaining Jedi from arena; opening land battle of Clone War; pursuit of Count Dooku; Obi-Wan, Anakin and then Yoda fight Dooku in lightsabre battles.

Distinguishing, first of all, between 'moments' and 'sequences', moments such as (i) have an immediate impact in terms of the story – in this case kick-starting the whole film – but can just as well remain plot progress points as in (v) where Obi-Wan is captured and therefore needs rescuing. Sequence (iv) provides us with a single moment of action but one that in its entirety exists as the core dramatic scene of the film. For all intents and purposes, however, (ii), (iii), (vi) and the successive climax (vii) are the major set-pieces understood in terms of action and spectacle. A particular feature of the *Star Wars* saga is its use of parallel lines of action in what has been termed 'Reel 6', the final twenty-five minutes or so of each of the films.[1] All contemporary action-adventure blockbusters, of course, climax with action. As established in *Jaws* and *A New Hope*, this works on two levels: the narrative conflict invariably resolved and the most impressive spectacle still fresh in audiences' senses as they leave the cinema. This is somewhat challenged in *The Empire Strikes Back* and the 'to be continued' nature of the prequels. The climaxes to *Return of the Jedi* (1983) and *The Phantom Menace*, however, provide for a mass of activity, crosscutting between three lines of action where one mission is very much dependent on the other. Where the characteristic *Star Wars* race or chase sequence provides for one form of spectacle, these parallel lines involve the three other main types of action used throughout the saga – a land battle, a space battle and a lightsabre battle. Reel 6 is the essence of organization, a feature of editing as much as storytelling but one that is nevertheless still based around very specific cause and effect. Progressing through an ebb and flow of stops and restarts, it tends to take the form of an impossible mission that gets worse before it gets better; the land mission to destroy the source of the force field, for example, going wrong before it is put right, leaving the space fighters to fend for themselves until they are finally able to destroy the target.

What is notable about Reel 6 of *Attack of the Clones*, however, is that it is successive rather than parallel. Whereas *Return of the Jedi* and *The Phantom Menace* see the main characters effectively split into separate missions, the climax to *Attack of the Clones* sees them come together after they have previously been parted. Even more classically cliffhanging, it is nevertheless strange to find a change in the expected formula and, without definite mission briefings, the successive cause and effect is much more unpredictable. As I have outlined in (vii), the film's climax goes through six escalating stages. The main protagonists defeat the monsters but the secessionist droids arrive. The Jedi Knights come to the rescue but then they are all close to defeat. Yoda and his Clone Army come to the rescue but Count Dooku escapes. Obi-Wan and Anakin find and fight him but are defeated. Yoda comes to the rescue but, in saving them, Dooku manages to get away. Ultimately, our heroes survive and the land battle is won but all of this with the air of a pyrrhic victory in what amounts to merely the beginning of the Clone War.

There is a narrative, or at least organizational, complexity going on here but also a narrative density. And this is the main factor that can be said to be compounded rather than assuaged by the digital special effects. This not only refers to the sheer mass of spectacle but also the detail. The characteristic complaint of the prequels is that the narrative is ultimately overburdened, the dialogue leaden and, in order to overcome accusations of flatness, the effects far too layered. The information overload – of narrative, action and spectacle – reaches its nadir in the gladiatorial arena, which comes to the point where the main protagonists, thousands of Geonosians, dozens of Jedi, three types of battle droid in their hundreds, and at least one of the remaining monsters, are all involved in battle. Yoda and the Clone Army then arrive from out of the sky and battle ships are brought into the equation. The opening land battle of the Clone War is itself very dense, various types of hardware from the one side fighting various types of hardware on the other. In order to offset the fact that what we are seeing apart from the principal actors is completely animated, the sequence is given deliberate realism in the form of zooms and pans, rumbling shakes of the virtual camera and almighty explosions that lead to smoke and dust as the droid and clone phalanxes march into each other. Only with the lightsabre battle, perhaps, does the story wrap on the level of character conflict. And it is left to the visual organization of the two final scenes to make the ironies felt, the Clone Army destroyers leaving Coruscant to fight for the Republic and the closing image of the newly married Anakin and Amidala framed in the same way as Luke and Leia at the end of *The Empire Strikes Back*. So, there is a combined aesthetic and narrative complexity throughout the film. But it could be said merely to serve the film and the saga's own internal dimensions.

<hr>

Case study 4

THE LORD OF THE RINGS: THE TWO TOWERS (2002)

One of the most recent developments in digital effects, CG characters provide us with a particular opportunity to square the circle with regard to spectacle versus narrative in live-action films and realism in computer-generated animation. Which is to say that defining them as essentially *animated* characters in *live-action* films completes the enquiry with regard to both spectacle and realism. These digital characters have been given several labels: cyberstars, synthespians, virtual actors, or, quite simply, vactors. Focusing on *Final Fantasy: The Spirits Within*, the first fully photorealistic CGA film, Steven Schleicher (2001) regards virtual actors as the 'final frontier' of 3D animation. Where digital aesthetics have successively colonized alien, mechanical and natural elements, the wholly believable simulation of characters relies on intricate physical details and textures, convincing movement, and the full range of emotional capabilities. Or, combining appearance, movement and expression, we need to be able to believe what we are seeing before we are able to follow these digital characters through given dramatic situations. CG characters take several forms. The human form is the ultimate application but with a wholly common sense argument as to why digital humans have yet to become fully fledged characters in live-action films: why generate a human in a central role when you can cast one? In live-action films, therefore, digital humans tend to be presented through composite and *en masse*. Composite refers to a number of methods relating to the replacement, manipulation and enhancement of an actor's existing performance. This becomes most apparent in superhuman moves that require digital stunt doubles, whether Neo fighting a hundred Agent Smiths in *The Matrix Reloaded* or Spider-Man swinging through New York. *En masse* refers to the fact that, for all intents and purposes, the true budgetary benefit of digital humans is that they can appear as extras, from passengers on the Titanic to the epic battle scenes in the *Lord of the Rings* trilogy.

It would be fair to state, therefore, that the main CG characters in live-action films remain creatures, monsters and mechanical beings: the T1000, Draco in *Dragonheart* (1996), Jar-Jar Binks, Sonny in *I, Robot* (2004), the titular stars of *Hulk* (2003) and *King Kong* (2005), and so on. This adds an important consideration to anything we may wish to say about digital humans. For Barbara Creed, the essential distinction is that

> [T]he presence of the synthespian in film is not meant to be perceived by the audience as a 'special effect' nor to draw attention to itself: the virtual or synthetic origins of the star will have to be rendered invisible by the text in order for the character to offer a convincing, believable performance. (Creed 2000: 83–4)

Which is to say that CG characters can't merely exist for themselves. Too apparent, and they exist as mere special effects; too realistic, then there is something too perfect about them. Perfection of the image always brings with it problems of depth. Even where this is addressed by adding deliberate imperfections, these characters still end up 'actors without an Unconscious' and this impacts enormously upon audience identification (Creed 2000: 84–5). So, the same factors come into play as the spectacle versus narrative argument, that we are to isolate CG characters – their technical origins, how they appear on screen, and so on – only to put them back into the full context of the films in which they appear. And with particular regard to CG characters used in science fiction and fantasy, we need to ask the same question previously applied to costume creatures and stop-motion monsters: namely, how are we to identify with characters that also exist as special effects?

The character of Gollum in the *Lord of the Rings* trilogy provides an example of a digital performance that is at once hidden and apparent. Seen only in glimpses in *The Fellowship of the Ring* (2001), it would be fair to state that his appearance in *The Two Towers* garnered just as much attention as the more obviously spectacular features in the film such as the fifteen-foot Ents and the epic battle for Helm's Deep. Indeed, appearing on magazine covers and having won the MTV Movie Award for Best Virtual Performance, Gollum has also become a fully fledged cyberstar. But in a film series composed of so many large-scale features, Gollum's distinctiveness lies in exactly the fact that he stands out as a focal point for essentially low-key spectacle. More central to the narrative, throughout the trilogy as a whole, than the Trolls, Balrog or Treebeard, he is a creature based entirely in characterization and given a combined appearance and performance that is curious, detailed and nuanced.

The technical requirements of this digital performance were such that it developed over all stages of writing, design, filming and postproduction. As Richard Taylor, WETA Workshop's Creative Supervisor, states of the technical demands of this iconic fantasy character: 'Gollum has almost become the statement of fantasy art in the twentieth century. So to be tasked with bringing Gollum to the screen as if he was a living, breathing creature was all-invading in our thoughts for a long time'.[2] Based on existing illustrations surrounding J.R.R. Tolkien's novels, Gollum first took the form of a marquette scanned onto computer in 1998. 'Cast' in terms of voice by actor Andy Serkis, the relative technical limitations early on in the process nevertheless matched the narrative requirement, that Gollum be seen only in shadow and outline in small parts of *The Fellowship of the Ring*. But the necessary progress for Gollum's fully fledged appearance in *The Two Towers* was made when Serkis went on to undertake an actual physical performance. Appearing in a white lycra suit, Serkis was shot on set as an animation reference, performing with the principal actors, and through the mime pass, removed from the central action and talking off screen. Essentially 're-cast' in 2001, the marquette Gollum was adapted to fit Serkis's facial expressions and physical performance. Combining both motion capture and more traditional key frame animation for nuances of movement and expression, further techniques followed in terms of rotoscoping and even painting, the former involving superimposing the digital Gollum over Serkis's performance and the latter effectively giving the character more textures. What is particularly notable about these technical factors is that Gollum represents a combination of elements beyond motion capture and pure digital imagery. Physically, technologically and emotionally, the result is what can only be described as a very layered performance.

As Mark J.P. Wolf argues, the potential problems with this digital performance are that it could be said to create a space of its own. Given more up-front screen time than the thousands of digital doubles in the film, this is entirely justified on dramatic grounds. But such is the success of the performance that it could be said to put other creature performances in the film to shame, whether the costumed orcs or the semi-animatronic Treebeard. As Wolf states:

> Compared to the smoothness of the digital effects, these older effects technologies do not appear as realistic. A strange kind of ontological shift occurs here; when we see the orc characters, we know they are actors in costume; but when we see Gollum, or the Balrog, it is just the character we are seeing, not an actor playing a character. The digital character exists on a separate plane, but it exists wholly on that plain, rather than being one kind of being attempting to be another, as in the case of the costumed actor. (Wolf 2003b: 56–7)

This is true to a certain extent but Gollum is arguably as much a composition, because a remediation, as costumed actors or animatronic creatures. Part of the success of the performance is that it covers its layered techniques so that we come to accept the technical novelty as a fully fledged performance and characterization. The contradiction, of course, is that we do know that there is an actor 'underneath' all of this, the result of so many magazine, television and DVD making-of features drawing attention to the technological construction of Gollum. The further success, therefore, is that we come to accept the character despite knowing more than we do about analogue effects that we've already simply come to accept. Principally, however, Gollum is taken out of his own aesthetic space by being thoroughly grounded in the ongoing narrative of the saga.

Like *Attack of the Clones*, in narrative terms *The Two Towers* is all middle. The Fellowship now having been split into three parts, Frodo and Sam continue their journey, Aragorn's narrative takes us to Helm's Deep, and Merry and Pippin's to the destruction of Isengard. Put into context, Gollum appears in the most modest but ultimately central strand, accompanying Frodo, Sam and the Ring to Mordor. Taking part in a narrative that is a journey, towards a destination rather than a battle, Gollum is essentially removed from large-scale spectacle and becomes the central spectacle, if you will, of that particular narrative. Digital in construction, more 'alien' in appearance, and given an aesthetic and a performance that provide for an off-centre realism, there is little doubt that Gollum stands out from the two costumed Hobbits played by Elijah Wood and Sean Astin. But his main function in the narrative is to combine two functions, to both help and hinder their journey. This becomes particularly manifest in the character's schizophrenia. Switching between his innocent (Smeagol) and corrupt (Gollum) selves, while this exercise in concentrated psychology makes Gollum even more of a curious and fascinating focus it also has an effect on the narrative and the other characters. Gollum therefore becomes the determining factor in whether the Hobbits will or will not reach Mordor, and his two selves simultaneously cause and reflect what appears to be the deteriorating relationship between the permanently hopeful Sam and the increasingly Ring-addicted Frodo.

Gollum appears in seven scenes in the extended DVD edition of *The Two Towers*. Having only previously been glimpsed and discussed, the first scene allows us to see this creature in full for the very first time. From out of the half light of the moon, we see him in both motion capture and motion control as he slopes down a ravine and grasps for the Ring. The Hobbits wake up and Sam wrestles the creature to the ground. It would be fair to state that, at this early stage at least, Gollum is more successfully realized in expressive close-up than in long and medium movement shots. He glides, too flatly, down the rock face and he is strong but essentially weightless in his scuffle with Sam. Which is to say that he is not yet successfully integrated into the existing, physical elements of the film. Environmental factors, however, go a long way to hiding any imperfections of movement and enhancing the detail and nuances of expression. Carefully introduced in the dark, the scene progresses to the light of the next day. A creature of nature, Gollum is almost chameleon in the ways in which his translucent skin comes to match the environments he appears in. Up close and in daylight, here we are first able to see Gollum's expressive capabilities as he flits between his young and ancient demeanours. It is principally the eyes and mouth, accompanied by hand movements, that work in presenting the hyperactive range of this quivering creature's feelings of excitement, fear and mistrust. In wider form, we then see him switch between biped and animal. He does agree to guide Frodo and Sam but he is as unstable as he is untrustworthy.

After finding an alternative route to Mordor and traversing the Dead Marshes, the fourth scene extends over day, night and the next day. From the grey marshes to the yellow-hued river, Gollum has found his ideal aesthetic match near water. The Hobbits discuss Gollum while he is hunting for fish, Sam's mistrust clashing with Frodo's empathy as Frodo starts to talk about the Ring in the same terms as Gollum. While the Hobbits sleep that night, Gollum is given a two-minute monologue that is also a dialogue between his two selves and is very much the key Gollum scene in technical and psychological terms. At this stage, halfway through the film, the camera is now up close and sustained. Sitting in the blue moonlit forest clearing, Gollum starts talking to himself as the camera slowly swings left and right. This sequence then becomes a series of edits as if between two characters, Gollum on the left speaking almost directly into the camera and Smeagol to the right talking down and to his right. Addiction to the Ring adds another aspect to Gollum's performance, the traumatic incident surrounding his initial possession of the Ring having led him to split into two conflicting selves and regaining possession promising a form of wholeness in the complete dominance of Gollum over Smeagol. The corrupt Gollum talks of killing the Hobbits and stealing the Ring, the innocent Smeagol almost talked into submission. Gollum sits relatively up straight and commands the screen with his mouth and eyes. Smeagol is hunched over with his eyes and mouth lowered. The camera moves in closer and closer to Gollum the more commanding he is until he accuses Smeagol of being a murderer. The camera then slowly moves in on Smeagol as he finds his resolve. 'Leave now, and never come back,' he says, and Gollum disappears.

This scene – effectively repeated as Gollum talks to his reflection in the lake in *The Return of the King* (2003) – is an excellent example of low-key spectacle. The nuances of expression, of the internal attempting to communicate outwards, are in themselves technically very accomplished but the scene also makes a greater impact in the context of filming and editing. By the end of the film Gollum has been freed from such formal framing and appears in a continuous two-minute steadicam shot. Deliberately lagging behind Frodo and Sam he stops to talk to himself again, to the left and right of the trees he stops at. This digital creature is given the last lines of the film. 'Smeagol will show you the way . . .' he says in his innocent voice; '. . . follow me,' says the sneering Gollum. The camera then pans up, back to the big picture, over the mountains towards Mordor.

Films, fans and the internet

The information surrounding certain films is often more important than the films themselves. Particularly in the case of blockbusters released on the back of trailers, television coverage, posters, magazine features and merchandising, Hollywood has colonized existing media with a highly visible and material efficiency. Although the internet has come to be used for similar methods of promotion it also works in 'reporting' on films in different ways, providing access to the latest news and gossip but remaining much more voluntary than existing media. The voluntary nature of the internet may well offer easy access for the browser, clicking on AOL's latest entertainment news in the same way that one might flick through a newspaper, for example. But the internet also exists as the most immediate, extensive and responsive outlet for information relating to film.

One of the problems in studying the internet is that it is a very fluid and constantly expanding source of information. When looking at the relationship between films and the internet, therefore, I will be focusing on areas of activity and levels of approach. In this chapter, I will be looking at the information surrounding films rather than actual films available on the internet. The potential for film content on the internet will be dealt with in the Conclusion. So what levels of approach can we bring to bear on film and the internet? There is a powerful distinction to be followed between film promotion on the one hand and fan activities on the other. In this chapter, I will be following this line of enquiry from studio output to fan input but in recent developments afforded by studies of both film promotion and film fandom, distinguishing between 'Film and the Internet' and 'The Internet and Film'. To start with film promotion is to assume a primary source of information. Traditional studies of film promotion have relied on the distinction between active and passive; studios fully in control of the dissemination of information about their products and audiences being regarded as mere recipients. Fan Studies, on the other hand, has tended to empower certain recipients, the financial 'push' of film promotion given more of an independent, passionate and playful 'pull' by fans of particular films, series and genres. In total, however, there is much more of a dialogue going on here, studios reliant upon interest and fans relying on particular film releases and the availability of information about them. Rather than looking at the situation in strict terms of 'official' and 'unofficial' uses of the internet, in this chapter I will be looking at the overall processes at work here, the main points of difference, dependence and independence.

Film and the internet

Film studios first began to take more than a passing interest in the promotional potential of the internet in the late 1990s. On one level, this was merely the film industry joining in with the 'internet boom' of the time. Prior to this point, however, the internet had already proven itself through grass roots activities. Constructed from without and settled from within, this is very much the story of the internet throughout the decade as a whole (see Chapter 1). From film message boards and newsgroups on the old Bulletin Board Service and Usenet systems, the advent of the World Wide Web enabled as much as it standardized, giving rise to thousands of increasingly interconnected fan sites and the more 'central' of the independent film websites such as IMDb, founded in 1990, and Corona Coming Attractions and Ain't It Cool News, both established in 1996. First of all, studios took notice of the number of fans who contributed to these sites, the seeming ease of access and response matched by knowledge of and passion over particular cult films and genres. Second, there were signs that early speculation, ongoing opinion and subsequent reviews on the internet were beginning to have an actual effect on the lead-up to and reception of certain films. The real-time nature of the internet is such that details surrounding films can be posted much earlier than existing media, in effect providing a longer period before the official press releases and media junkets. This process and the ways in which speculation follows speculation can be said to give films even greater coverage and expectation or, conversely, increase the length of time when potentially damaging 'word of mouse' can take hold.

As Harry Knowles, founder of Ain't It Cool, recounts, 1997 was a key year in terms of the film industry, film journalism and the media as a whole taking note of this new form of film reporting. Having received the script and creature designs for Paul Verhoeven's forthcoming *Starship Troopers* (1997) from the first of his many studio 'spies', Knowles was ordered to remove the material from his website by Sony. Lobbied by the film's producers seeing this as more of a publicity coup, however, Sony recanted and in what Knowles recounts as a 'geek' David versus 'corporate' Goliath battle, Ain't It Cool went on to gather more visitors and evoke interest from film journalists who understood that Knowles was in the same business as they were and yet, very possibly, represented the next development of that business. Other notable scoops from the early years of Ain't It Cool include a favourable preview of *Titanic* and allegedly damaging reviews of *Batman and Robin* (1997) and *Godzilla* (Knowles 2002: 114–20).

Film sites

Entering into this new matrix of film news, reviews and opinion, official film sites can be said to work in three ways:

(i)   to provide news, images and information on forthcoming releases direct from the source of production, as a central source of promotion and without recourse to existing media;

(ii) to act as the official source for information taken up by existing media and film websites; and

(iii) to 'channel' fan activities, effectively feeding fans' interest and attempting to limit any damaging effects on their films. This can be done in several ways, from simply acting as an efficient outlet to allowing images and information to be used by other sites which they are either obliged to source or to which they must provide a hyperlink back to the official site.

Most official film sites provide a very basic approach to form and content, their concern for replicating the flavour of the film often falling short of a full reflection due to the need to present the casual user with clarity of design and ease of navigation. While some sites include special features such as games and chat rooms, most sites provide only the standard features such as Story, Cast and Crew, Photo Gallery, Behind the Scenes, Video Clips, Trailer and Downloads. Given this standardization, academic accounts of official film sites tend to focus on the exceptions as opposed to the rule, especially, in recent historical terms, the key sites and allied campaigns that have become the benchmarks for sophisticated film promotion on the internet. These are the sites that go beyond superficial design, and act as creative reflections and extensions of the designated films, taking users much further into the world of the film or, in the case of science fiction and fantasy, into the wider 'universe' of the films. Inasmuch as we can separate them, there are two processes going on here, the user becoming more involved with the film itself, and aspects of the narrative of the film finding further space online.

In his analysis of the official *Blair Witch Project* website, J.P. Telotte (2001) provides a model account of a combined film, site and campaign. As Telotte states, blairwitch.com wasn't the only factor in raising awareness of the film. But one of its many notable features is that both 'online' and 'offline' campaigns shared the same strategy in blurring the distinction between reality and fiction as fostered by the film itself. Compared with other horror-themed sites from the same year, the *Blair Witch* site also demonstrated the same independence as the film. Where these other sites provided information on the films and the horror tradition of which they were part, the *Blair Witch* site was much less film-referential or film-industrial in what it did and worked in creating a convincing back-story to the film. Split up into The Legend, The Filmmakers and The Aftermath, a narrative world was created that brought the historical into line with the contemporary, the film based on the footage shot by three student filmmakers who went missing while investigating the Blair Witch legend. Telotte makes use of Janet H. Murray's (1997) consideration of 'immersion', 'agency' and 'transformation' in analysing the site. Given a certain degree of atmosphere, the site takes users further into the world of Burkitsville through histories, maps, police reports, video footage and so on. Agency arises through the user being able actively to navigate this jigsaw-like material and delve deeper into the mystery through Heather's diary and other personal recollections. The three-way, first-person perspective of *The Blair Witch Project* goes a long way to carrying the sense of immersion into the film itself but primarily the film takes over and gathers much of its effect from the loss of agency. Unlike the website, we are not in control of which perspective to follow and so certain things remain hidden from us. Ultimately, therefore, interest and involvement give way to the transformative effects of identification and empathy. We may well get lost in the woods along with the filmmakers, but it is not truly us who go missing.

Networks

Individual sites have been analysed in terms of the parallel or further depth they bring to a film. This has been followed through to sites promoting narratively complex films such as *Requiem for a Dream* (2000) and *Donnie Darko* (2001) (Beck 2004). Recent promotional strategies have come to take advantage of the live, continuous and network qualities of the internet. As Will Brooker and John T. Caldwell argue, official websites try to remain centres of information by also becoming greater centres of activity. It could well be, therefore, that narrative complexity and a greater sense of involvement are merely techniques for keeping users here, at this site, as opposed to any other. Principally referring to television, Brooker and Caldwell look at the ways in which programmers actively seek to create an after-hours audience, to have viewers log on straight after transmission in order to create, and in many ways contain, fandom. Caldwell looks at 'TV/dot-com' sites such as *Homicide*, *Freakylinks*, *Dawson's Creek*, *Futurama* and *Sex and the City*, all of which successfully 'herded' otherwise 'grazing' audiences into their fold (Caldwell 2003: 141). He terms this 'second-shift media aesthetics'. Where the 'first-shift' principally revolved around scheduling, the 'second-shift' represents the attempt to bring viewers back to series whose otherwise smooth scheduling has been cut into by increased competition, video recorders, and so on. One answer, therefore, is that if viewers tune in again next week they will also be able to log on and discuss what they've seen with similarly inclined viewers. Looking more closely at his chosen programme, the British series *Attachments*, Brooker terms this 'overflow'. Examining the situation first in terms of top-down as opposed to bottom-up fandom, Brooker then charts the continuation of the programme's associated website, Seethru, after the programme had been cancelled. This was done through the express needs of fans of the series and the willingness by the production company to keep the site going, in many ways a more 'egalitarian relationship between producers and their audiences' (Brooker 2003: 333).

The example of television works in these instances because it is itself a relatively live and continuous medium. Indeed, reality television shows such as *Big Brother* and *Survivor* make this particularly manifest through the use of phone votes and continuous coverage on digital television and the internet. Official film sites are too specific, perhaps, to fit fully into the live principal of overflow but they are continuous insofar as they are able to follow films from pre-production to release. They are also commonly associated with a network of sites. The standard network sites are the 'hub' studio sites. The largest, such as sony.com, warnerbros.com and universalpictures. com, are corporate in both design and intent, clean, well organized and with the minimum of fuss beyond side ads and scrolling posters. Starting with the home page, users are first presented with the entirety of outlets and products. Warner Bros Online, for example, offers Movies, Television, Music, DVD, Games, Kids and Win! Such a site is clearly aimed at the casual user, the family-based film and television viewer, and offers all that the viewer-consumer needs under one roof. The aim of the site, therefore, is to keep the user in Warner world. Clicking on Kids, for example, leads to Harry Potter, The WB, Scooby Doo, DC Comics and Loony Toons. Clicking on Movies on all of these mall-like studio sites takes the user straight to the latest releases, forthcoming releases, cinema chains and film showings, and with the opportunity to click on film titles or posters in order to access the official film sites themselves.

Film franchises provide us with the most continuous, sustained and networked sites: relatively continuous at the level of production and, as we'll see in the next section, taking part in a developing network of fan reliance and resistance. But what about films like *The Blair Witch Project*, which are for all intents and purposes one-offs? One other notable film site since blairwitch.com has been that for Steven Spielberg's *A.I.: Artificial Intelligence* (2001). The backstory provided by the site revolved around (i) the 'gestation' of the robot David, in real time, in the six months up to the release of the film, and (ii) a murder mystery involving 'sentient machine therapist' Jeanine Salla and a character named Evan Chan. Where the former saw David being born in time for the film, the latter ended with the killer – and the link with the film – being revealed. What helped make this narrative so continuous was the fact that aimovie.com also contained links to other sites, some existing sites such as the American Association for Artificial Intelligence and the chance to converse with existing AI programme, ALICE, but others fictional and set in a wholly speculative, future backdrop to the world of the film. Such sites included the Coalition for Robotic Freedom Homepage and the Sentient Property Crime Bureau. The user's first way in to the murder mystery was through the trailer for the film released on the site. Featuring a credit for Jeanine Salla, anyone then typing her name into Google was directed to the Bangalore University Home Page. An alternative way in to the mystery was provided by anyone who decoded the notched letters that appeared throughout the trailer. Transferred into numbers, they presented the enquiring user with a phone number that led to an answer machine message. The murder mystery could also be followed through regular email updates (see Haley 2001; Brooker 2003; Pullen 2004). A cerebral, puzzle-solving campaign, it demonstrated the beginnings of a technological overflow that, while not yet as organized, has partly come to work through the ability to access promotional information via email, iPod and mobile phone updates. Regarded in these terms, it may well come to a point when information about films could become as involuntary as glancing posters on the sides of buses. There might be no need to search out the information because it will come looking for you.

The internet and film

We have already looked at some of the ways in which consideration of the television viewer, internet user and videogame player can be said to have cut into singular and previously privileged notions of the cinema spectator (see Chapter 1). In truth, since its formation as an identifiable, multidisciplinary field in the 1990s, Audience Studies has always been democratic, willing to refine outdated notions of the passive and the duped and instead look to the newly active and interactive as the respective 'audiences' of different media have themselves come to converge. Where Television Audience Studies had its basis in Anglo-American cultural studies – that is, the study of actual people's viewing habits – the study of cinema audiences began with variations on reader-response criticism, psychoanalysis, and the Marxist view that the apparatus of cinema is merely an extension of the state apparatus. As Judith Mayne (1993) and others have argued, the theoretical ruminations of Jean-Louis Baudry, Raymond Bellour, Christian Metz *et al.* did bring attention round to the subject of cinema audiences. But they did so in such a way as to squeeze actual people out of the equation and impose upon them a top-down model that recast cinema as an 'institution' and spectators as 'subjects'. More recent approaches have come to favour the bottom-up, cutting through the generalization of such institutional models and instead asking specific questions about real people and particular choices relating to different types of films (see also Cook and Bernink 1999: 366–73; Stokes and Maltby 2001; Brooker and Jermyn 2003: 127–66).

Fan studies

Initially benefiting from the more democratic approach to audiences, what has come to be known as Fan Studies can be regarded as a particular offshoot of Audience Studies. As John Fiske states:

> Fandom is a common feature of popular culture in industrial societies. It selects from the repertoire of mass-produced and mass-distributed enter-tainment certain performers, narratives or genres and takes them into the culture of a self-selected fraction of people. They are then reworked into an intensely pleasurable, intensely signifying popular culture that is both similar to, yet significantly different from, the culture of more 'normal' popular audiences. (Fiske 1992: 30)

This notion of same-but-different is very appropriate when approaching Fan Studies. If we regard the study of fans as being part of Audience Studies, then there is a problem in the fact that fans tend to be regarded as much more alternative and active than mainstream audiences. More discerning in their choice of texts, film and televi-sion, fans have been distinguished from 'mere' viewers in several ways. Apart from simply watching, fans purchase, engage with, appropriate, interrogate, share, communicate, debate and create. They pre-view and constantly re-view their chosen texts, and seek out and exchange all possible information relating to those texts. At their most committed and organized, fans are said to represent a definite community of interest and, having mined all of the existing releases, transmissions and information, go on to create their own extensions of their favoured texts. In short, they are regarded as more actively active than mainstream audiences.

There are a number of ways to redress this initial imbalance: first, looking at what Fan Studies has become independent of Audience Studies and, second, the ways in which the internet has recently come to problematize the distinction between fans and audiences. In Kirsten Pullen's excellent survey of Fan Studies, she starts with the argument that fans are drawn to texts that are said to be more open to interpretation than mainstream texts. Science fiction and fantasy series have tended to garner the most fan worship because they are based on continual narratives in imaginative worlds that open up a universe of possibilities for further intervention. The most studied television series in this respect include *Star Trek*, *Doctor Who*, *The Prisoner*, *Blake's 7*, *The X-Files*, *Babylon 5*, *Xena: Warrior Princess* and *Buffy the Vampire Slayer* (see Bacon-Smith 1992; Jenkins 1992; Tulloch and Jenkins 1995; Pullen 2000; Lancaster 2001; Lancaster and Mikotowicz 2001; Hills 2001 and 2002). If this acts as a definition of the texts that fans tend to favour, almost as a matter of narrative fact, the problem with traditional Fan Studies, argues Pullen, is that it tended to over-romanticize fandom. Choosing certain texts 'because they see something in them that critics and the mainstream audience have missed', fans are said to go on to form 'an alternative community which rebels against mainstream norms and creates a space for open communication of liberal, democratic ideals' (Pullen 2004: 83).

Originally envisaged as more alternative and democratic than mainstream audiences, while the distinction between active fans and passive audiences existed as a useful starting point, Fan Studies has grown to such an extent that it has developed its own internal approaches and arguments. Like Audience Studies, in fact, Fan Studies is caught between notions of commonality and diversity; that there are certain things that can be said to define fans but there are also many types of people, interests and activities within that. How are we to distinguish the Elvis impersonator from the comic book collector, for example, or the sports fan from the soap opera fan (see Lewis 1992; Harris and Alexander 1998; Hills 2002)? Film and television fandom contains its own internal conflicts such as *Buffy* fans versus *Charmed* fans and *Star Wars* versus *Matrix* fans. The fact that film and television fandom have grown so much in recent years, however, has come to provide another potential conflict. At what point does fandom become mainstream? While early accounts of fandom were able to make the case for more discerning fan activities in the time of mail order, fan clubs and bootleg tapes, principally through the internet we now all have access to information surrounding films and television programmes. This has the potential to make fans of us all.

Online fandom

While the notion of fandom for all can be welcomed for reducing the distinction between fans and audiences, it begs the question: what accounts for genuine fandom on the internet? As highlighted in the previous section, fandom is particularly instructive when applied to film trilogies and series such as *Star Wars*, *Lord of the Rings*, *The Matrix*, *Harry Potter* and *Spider-Man*. The closest to anything we may say about the continual nature of television, these are commercial franchises that fulfil the textual requisite of offering imaginary worlds that can be expanded in both official and unofficial directions. In their analysis of internet discussion groups up to nine months before the release of *The Fellowship of the Ring*, Bertha Chin and Jonathan Gray look at the ways in which fans act as constant 'pre-viewers' of their favoured texts, a situation only possible approaching this first film because those pre-viewers were essentially fans of the books. Primarily, Chin and Gray are interested in the expanded horizons of textuality here. Pre-viewing a 'pre-text' might well be based on its own internal logic but such discussion also 'creates a framework for interpretation of the *Lord of the Rings* films post-release' (Chin and Gray 2001: 2). That is, how successful has Peter Jackson been in adapting the material? How will this translate across the whole trilogy? And will the films create fans who will then go on to read the books? Chin and Gray divide the responses into: (i) the Tolkien purists opposed to any form of adaptation; (ii) the hesitant but hopeful; and (iii) those positively excited by the prospect of the forthcoming film. As Chin and Gray conclude, although these postings lack the sense of a classic virtual community – developing a language of its own and branching off into personal discussion – there is a definite sense of a textual community here, fans of the books naturally protective of their common interest.

If this speaks to the communicative potential of the internet, the creative aspect of fandom has best come to be exemplified through the rise of fan films. To a large extent, fan films represent an extension of fan fiction. Much discussed throughout the 1990s, fan fiction acts as a creative and often alternative extension of fans' favoured texts, with 'filk' and 'slash' fiction, in particular, working to subvert the original texts' usual white, male, heterosexual bias. The internet has made fan fiction more available but fan films take advantage of the full video and audio capabilities of the internet. As Henry Jenkins (2003) argues in his particular focus on *Star Wars* fan films, they represent a potential 'third space' between top-down media convergence and bottom-up fan culture. Taking advantage of the DIY opportunities of digital filmmaking and using the internet as the primary means of distribution, the films are rough and polished, serious and playful, and while the *Star Wars* fan films, in particular, are very much beholden to the saga and its creator, they also demonstrate an independent spirit that is not afraid to poke fun at either Lucas, the films (especially the prequels) or the nature of fandom itself (see also Brooker 2002: 173–97; Jones 2002).

In the following case studies, I will be combining the main points raised in this and the previous section by looking at fans' relationship with their favoured films. Based primarily on their responses to the official trailers, first, I will examine *Star Wars* fans' pre-viewing of the 'final' entry in the saga, *Revenge of the Sith*, then I will look at responses to the release of the graphic novel adaptation, *Sin City*. These case studies will focus on the organized fan sites: The Force.Net and Superhero Hype. I will be exploring: the ways in which fans communicate on fan forums; the topics raised and the opinions expressed; and, ultimately, the 'value' of such communication on the internet.

Case study 5

STAR WARS EPISODE III: REVENGE OF THE SITH (2005)

Avowed *Star Wars* scholar-fan, Will Brooker, has produced work that bridges old and new fan activities, from early fanzines and slash fiction to fan sites and fan films. Writing before the release of the twentieth-anniversary Special Editions, Brooker (1997) distinguishes between the official and the unofficial in terms of merchandising and fandom. Overstated in this particular instance, Brooker casts the distinction in terms of the narrative of the films: namely, the Rebel Alliance of fans providing alternative materials and activities to the officially sanctioned commercial goods of the Lucasfilm Empire and its print licencees, Bantam and Boxtree, Marvel and DC. Writing before the release of *Attack of the Clones*, Brooker is able to add more perspective to the ethos as it applies to more recent attitudes and activities. First of all, current *Star Wars* fandom cannot but help be informed by the generational divide inherent in the thirty-year span of the series, or, providing further perspective to arguments raised in Chapter 3, the ways in which the prequels can be said to have inadvertently added to the valorization of the original trilogy. The original fans, of the original trilogy, regard the prequels in very much the same way that critics regarded the originals, that, without a similar lapse of time, we're back to soulless spectacle and manipulative merchandising. This takes several levels – nostalgia, for one – but technology has a lot to do with it, in a recasting of the spectacle versus narrative argument that George Lucas has essentially ignored the storytelling properties of the saga in favour of digital excess. The same can also be said of what might be termed digital fandom, that for the original fans, while the avenues of communication are greater, those avenues are open to far too many and the far too young (Brooker 2002: 79–99 and 221–37). In total, however, fandom and the franchise have developed so much that there is more correctly an inter-dependence going on between the two, an opposition that is also an appropriation and further expansion of the saga.

TheForce.Net (TFN) is the most established of the thousands of *Star Wars* fan sites available on the internet.[1] Since its formation in 1998 it has developed into an extensive database of news, opinion and fan-related activities, with over 192,000 members currently registered for the Jedi Council Forum message boards (June 2005). In many ways, it is the most official of the unofficial *Star Wars* fan sites. TFN maintains an abiding relationship with Lucasfilm Ltd (LFL) and covers all aspects of the franchise. Four of its twelve main sections, for example, are specifically devoted to Star Wars TV, Videogames, Books and Comic Books. The site can only truly thrive, however, through input from fans themselves. Six of the remaining sections on the site are entirely devoted to fan contributions and activities: FanForce (news and events from *Star Wars* 'chapters' around the world), Humour, Fan Art, Collecting, Fan Fiction and Fan Films. Covering the run-up to, and reception of all the *Star Wars* prequels, TFN is ideal with regard to my ongoing argument because it covers both official and unofficial avenues. As Will Brooker details through extensive use of TFN, specific speculation surrounding *Attack of the Clones* started as soon as *The Phantom Menace* had been released. This speculation took many forms, from early images and conjecture surrounding the title to 'leaked' plot points and 'fake' scripts (Brooker 2002: 115–28). There is as much, if not more, concern for narrative than matters of action, design and spectacle in

Star Wars fans' expectations. Throughout the prequels this has developed its own narrative, principally the hope that the next prequel will be better than the previous one. For many, therefore, *Revenge of the Sith* was the last chance to redeem the prequels. As a focus for the lead-up to Episode III, I will be focusing on fan reactions to the two main trailers for the film.

Trailers have proven the ideal promotional tool for release on the internet. The aim of trailers is to provide audiences with a preview of forthcoming attractions. Initially used exclusively in cinemas, they have since gone on to be shown on television and now the internet. However much they can now be seen out of place, their aim is still very much the same, used as part of the overall campaign to create early interest in forthcoming cinema releases. The first trailer to be premiered online was the teaser trailer for *The Phantom Menace*. Teaser trailers are the earliest possible glimpse of a film which is then followed by the main 'theatrical' trailer – or trailer B – aired closer to the release of the film. The internet premiere for *The Phantom Menace* was significant in a number of ways. For fans, it was the first glimpse of moving images from the first new *Star Wars* film for over fifteen years. In seven days, 1.5 million fans downloaded the teaser and, proving itself the first ever internet-related film 'event', it has now become the standard film industrial approach to releasing trailers. This is not to forget the appeal of trailers shown in cinemas. *Star Wars* fans found themselves going to films like *Meet Joe Black*, *The Waterboy* and *The Siege* primarily to see the *Phantom Menace* trailers. But viewing trailers online makes it into more of an activity, logging on and downloading as appropriate, and seeing it *first* also becomes a matter of watching it as many times as desired and discussing it with fellow fans. Trailers have also proven the ideal promotional tool on the internet because they are essentially two-minute windows that fulfil all of the requirements of the Quicktime mentality, small enough in time and size to be downloaded and pored over frame by frame. What they lack in terms of the big screen they make up for in terms of repeated viewing and intense deconstruction.

The teaser trailer for *Revenge of the Sith* was released on 4 November 2004. An event in itself, the release of trailers on the internet has now become thoroughly coordinated with other outlets, providing a promotional overflow across a wide range of media. The trailer was first made available to Hyperspace subscribers on starwars.com and AOL users. It was then premiered on television in the evening editions of *Access Hollywood* and MTV's *Total Request Live*. On the following day, the trailer was shown during similar entertainment programmes worldwide, premiered at cinemas with showings of *The Incredibles*, and made available to Orange mobile phone customers. The teaser trailer then became free for all to watch on starwars.com on 8 November. Following similar lines, the main theatrical trailer was premiered on 10 March 2005 during the commercials to *The*

O.C. and made available to Hyperspace subscribers immediately afterwards, becoming free for all on 14 March. The previous sense of internet exclusivity is now contradicted somewhat by the number of exclusives across other media. But the new draw is exactly that of confined time and expanded space, *when* to see the trailers complemented by *where* they can be found. For its part, the internet remains the only permanent source and does retain its sense of exclusivity when compared to the more public outlets of television and cinema. Helping with this treasure hunt aspect, TFN posted constant news as to the trailers' availability, stretching back to the very first images released as flash ads on starwars.com on 2 November. Unable actually to show the teaser trailer, TFN produced its own montage of images on the eve of its release. Immediately removed on request from LFL, two hours later TFN posted a frame-by-frame description of the 1 minute 36 second trailer.

Fan expectations and reactions can be traced through the twenty-nine threads devoted to the trailers on the *Revenge of the Sith* board of TFN's Jedi Council Forums. Taking place between 2 November 2004 and 22 March 2005, essentially the posts can be divided between: those waiting to see the two trailers; those who have seen the trailers; and queries and advice relating to how and where to see them. The responses to the trailers primarily pick up on: their construction; the appearance of characters; glimpses of action; snippets of dialogue; and the look of featured planets. They also work in trying to piece together the narrative of the film, principally who fights who (and when) in the numerous lightsabre duels and exactly how Anakin turns to the Dark Side and becomes Darth Vader.

The most substantive discussion surrounding the trailers is engendered by the nature of their release on the internet. This can be deduced from the number of posts, length of the responses, and what might be termed depth of feeling. Started by Master_Obi-Wan a week before the release of the main trailer, the 'Next Week: File-sharing and the full trailer – allowed or taboo?' (3/3/05) thread picks up on LFL's reiteration of copyright in terms of downloading the trailer, posting it on other sites and making the trailer available for file-share:

> The trailer is copyright material of Lucasfilm with exclusive distribution online at starwars.com and on AOL.
>
> We expect theforce.net and other fan sites to honor Lucasfilm's rights on this material.
>
> At the same time, you know you will be able to catch it on TV, watch it in the theaters, have a preview on Hyperspace and see it for free online starting the following Monday. That's a lot of opportunities. (Ghent, 3/3/05)

Responses variously point out that once the trailer has been aired on television it becomes public property, disagree with LFL's attempts to police the internet, and regard it as a particular insult to fans. As Crimson_Empire, for example, writes:

> Your kidding right?
>
> Are you aware that there are about 2 zillion threads with copyrighted pics in them on this site RIGHT NOW?
>
> TFN needs to drop the captain kiss a__ routine.
>
> I love Lucas to death, and worship his movies, and will be downloading the first copy of the trailer, legal or not when it comes out. And I will not feel any shame.
>
> Seriously. People are out there right now, shooting people and kicking puppies. The LAST thing I am gonna punish myself for is being addicted to Star Wars.
>
> Downloading a trailer early hurts NOBODY. These 'exclusives' are designed for big corporations to hoover up yer dollars anyway. It's not about us. (3/3/05)

Following the argument that fandom needs to be free, some members use the language of *Star Wars* in order to make their feelings felt. As DarthHutt, for example, writes: 'The more you tighten your grip LFL, the more Hyperspace members will slip through your fingers' (4/3/05). In an involved thread that goes on to talk about the difficulty of policing the internet and the sheer availability, in any case, of the trailers, opposition takes the form of exposing the full range of contradictions that appear to be at work here. Many fans pick up on the contradiction inherent in the fact that Hyperspace members are being robbed of their sense of exclusivity in an overall multimedia campaign that will see the trailer first aired on television and then through numerous other outlets. As ronthebassman writes:

> Hyperspace has turned out to be a failed attempt at fan relations that has done more damage than good. Who in their right mind is going to renew their subscription? I sure as hell won't! Not to draw a comparison or anything . . . but check out http://www.kongisking.net to see how Peter Jackson is treating HIS fans! (4/3/05)

It is, therefore, left to the forum moderators to try to ease the situation. Balanced in terms of both giving their reasons for abiding by the ruling and remaining good-humoured, they remind the fans why they are there and why they care. As moderator, Darth Sapient, writes:

SW Fan: I can't believe Lucas is running the trailer during the OC. I paid for HS. What a slap in the face!!!!

Logs off.

Watches the OC.

SW Fan: Man, that was awesome. Lucas is listening to his fans. The duel is like we've always wanted. He rocks. Thank you, Lucas. (4/4/03)

For those outside fandom in general and *Star Wars* fandom in particular, such a thread could be regarded as merely 'obsessive', the ease of response online merely compounding the situation. But such a thread is instructive in that the responses can also be regarded as 'impassioned' and represent a sort of meta-commentary whereby it is not only *Star Wars* fandom or fandom in general that is at stake but also the particularities of online fandom.

Case study 6

SIN CITY (2005)

We are currently undergoing a definite wave of comic book and graphic novel adaptations. Although there have been comic book adaptations before, most notably around the time of DC's *Superman* (1978–87) and *Batman* (1989–97) films, never have they appeared so consistently over a definite number of years. It was principally the success of *X-Men* (2000) and *Spider-Man* (2002) that demonstrated the commercial viability of superhero films, and other box-office successes have included: *X-Men 2* (2003), *Spider-Man 2* (2004), *Batman Begins* (2005), *Superman Returns* (2006) and *X-Men 3* (2006). With DC having already used its most recognizable icons, Marvel spent much of the 1980s and 1990s trying to rescue its back catalogue from television rights. Ultimately, however, this delay proved advantageous with regard to the fact that we are now able to see digitally realized super-heroes doing on screen what they've never been able to do before. The timing has also proven advantageous with regard to the internet providing evidence of a notable fanbase from which to launch these expensive and initially unproven adaptations. Comic book fans had been ruminating upon several unmade projects on the internet since the mid-1990s, including Tim Burton's *Superman Lives* and James Cameron's version of *Spider-Man*. Fundamentally driven by the notion of faithfulness, comic book fans have questioned forthcoming adaptations in the following areas: choice of director; casting; costume design; and, essentially, any tampering whatsoever with the iconic characters and events of their favourite superhero comic books. For many directors taking on such material, therefore, trying to redress this initial scepticism is very much the touchstone for their adaptations, that comic book fans will come to accept the necessary changes and subsequently become fans of the films (see, for example, Thompson 2002; Hughes 2003).

For their part, graphic novels exist exactly in order to make changes. A product of both the economic downturn in comic book sales in the 1980s and writer-illustrators who had grown up with comic books, graphic novels are distinguished in terms of their more 'literary' storylines, 'realistic' characters and 'adult' approach. Beginning with Alan Moore and Dave Gibbons's *Watchmen*, and Frank Miller's *Batman: The Dark Knight Returns*, in 1986, they either provide for original material or work in updating the iconography and *modus operandi* of existing superhero characters. They also work in disposing of the notion of superheroes altogether by tackling other genres such as crime and horror. Fans of graphic novels are invariably fans of comic books but arguably see themselves as more discerning and it is not so much the serial superhero characters that they follow as the main *auteurs* who lend their particular vision to all the genres they work within. To date, the main graphic novel adaptations have been: three films based on Alan Moore's work, *From Hell* (2001), *The League of Extraordinary Gentlemen* (2003) and *V for Vendetta* (2005); Max Allan Collins's *Road to Perdition* (2002); John Wagner's *A History of Violence* (2005); and Frank Miller's *Sin City*.

Like TheForce.Net, Superhero Hype (SHH) is the most organized and extensive site devoted to comic books and comic book adaptations.[2] Run in association with Coming Soon and Crave Online Media, it is part of a network of sites devoted to film, television, videogames, music and comics. Focused on the particular theme of superheroes, SHH benefits from being part of this network because it is essentially concerned with comic books and graphic novels adapted across a range of media. Upon entering the site, one is able to access Heroes, News, Features, Boards, Media, Products and Fan Reviews. Like TFN, the site combines official news and an interest in commercial products with input from fans. SHH contains six general message boards devoted to different media and fifteen devoted to specific superheroes. The site consists of over 21,000 registered members and with stats for the current boards including 104,000 threads made up of over 4,500,000 posts (June 2005). With particular regard to graphic novels, two of the Hero boards are devoted to *Sin City* and *V for Vendetta*. The Sin City board comprises four forums: Sin City (the film); The Comics; Sin City 2; and Sin City Sequels. The Sin City film forum is the largest, with 640 threads made up of over 13,000 posts.

We have already looked at the ways in which fandom undergoes 'development', that, in the case of a long-standing saga such as *Star Wars*, any new entry into the film or product canon will be met by a pre-existing fandom and a continuation of that fandom. When it comes to comic book and graphic novel adaptations, there is more correctly what may be termed 'transferral'. As we have seen in relation to the *Lord of the Rings* films, the initial scrutiny is that from fans of the original published material. Frank Miller's *Sin City* was published in nine volumes from 1991 to 1999. The *Sin City* film was directed by Robert Rodriguez in association with Miller. Based on three of the first volumes, *The Hard Goodbye*, *The Big Fat Kill* and *That Yellow Bastard*, the film has been regarded as the most faithful of graphic novel adaptations. This applies not only to the script but also, fundamentally, the look of the movie, filmed on virtual sets and making particular use of black, white and striking dashes of colour.

While this faithfulness is very much applauded in the Sin City forum, the actors are judged on their appearance in two ways: how they look in relation to their characters and, quite simply, how they look. The latter becomes particularly evident in 'The I LOVE CLIVE OWEN thread' and 'Miho appreciation thread!!!'. As Susan Clerc (1996) has outlined, so-called appreciation threads are a continuation of similar attitudes to stars and celebrities offline. As Clerc argues, although there might well be an assumed male bias in such posts, for every male fan lusting after actress Gillian Anderson in *The X-Files*, for example, there are almost as many female fans devoted to David Duchovny. The SHH forums make extensive use of images and links. It is in this respect that pictures of the characters in the Sin City appreciation threads give way to links relating to the actors and actresses in other roles and appearances. This is particularly noticeable in the Miho thread which, while it begins with images from the film, quickly moves onto shots and links of model-turned-actress Devon Aoki from other sources. The four threads devoted to Jessica Alba are most symptomatic of appearance over performance. The threads barely even mention her character at all, much less her actual performance, and her appearance extends to her appearances as fans hunt for all possible images of this young starlet: 'Jessica Alba Needs Her OWN DVD Cover Damn It' , 'Jessica Alba on the cover of "Rolling Stone"!!!', 'Autographed Nancy Pic!', 'Jessica Alba @ MTV Movie Awards last night'.

Although the point is rarely made, a lot of communication in fan forums isn't necessarily of substantive value. Although tightly contained in early newsgroups – and, even more so, academic readings of those groups – a large fan site such as SHH clearly takes us into the sort of general internet fandom identified by Kirsten Pullen (2004), in this case ostensible *Sin City* fans talking about Jessica Alba on MTV. Such posts come to tell us as much about celebrity culture in general as online fan cultures in particular. Too specialist, perhaps, and fan sites simply exist for themselves. In searching for Frank Miller fan sites, for example, there are only those that impart basic information, and those launched on the back of the *Sin City* film are too recent to have developed a notable community.[3] Where SHH provides us with a general fandom, it does nevertheless provide us with a way to understand some of the current particularities of the internet. There is little doubt, for example, that it is determined by age, SHH being primarily composed of teenagers and early twenty-somethings.[4] There is also another way of understanding 'appearance' that goes beyond 'appreciation'. This provides a much more interesting, digital-savvy variation on fandom, one that counters simple opinion and access to images through the *production* of images. The most recognizable form is that of fans dressing up as their favourite characters. Familiar from sci-fi and comic book conventions, here it refers to posting pictures online, as in the case of Michelle's thread on the Sin City forum, 'My Nancy Costume!' (10/7/05). This is a form of masquerade that has been valued in terms of identification and emulation, in this case a visual representation of the play on identities allowed within the context of virtual communities. The next step on from this, however, is the ability to alter digital photos which are then posted online. This is evident in the most popular thread in the Sin City forum, 'Show us your Pic, Sin City Style!!' (3/4/05). Started by punisherchick and having received over 400 replies, here members either alter their photos so that they appear as specific characters or, remaining themselves, make use of the *Sin City* style in terms of colour, fonts and panels. This demonstrates a particularly creative, visual input principally from readers and fans of the graphic novels.

Ultimately, a mainstream fan site like SHH is more of a test case for fandom rather than a given, but one that nevertheless provides us with a wide enough audience to help specify certain claims. How are we to distinguish, for example, between general users of this superhero site and readers, viewers and fans of *Sin City*? Are fans of the graphic novels automatically fans of the film and does the film create fans of the graphic novels? As Jonathan Gray (2003) argues, Audience Studies and Fan Studies have come to share much of the same language in recent years, ignoring what might be termed 'non-fans' and even 'anti-fans'. Although it is something of an automatic assumption, I do believe that the self-styled *Sin City* pictures outlined above evidence a specific fandom resulting out of the graphic novels, not merely in the activity but also the faithfulness of design. At the very least, there is knowledge and creativity at work here. But what of discussion? Fans air their opinions online but so do non-fans. The most substantive thread on the Sin City forum in terms of issues and discussing the film in-depth is 'Sin City? Sexist City' (16/4/05). What is particularly interesting about this thread are the ways in which responses follow not only in terms of the arguments *per se* but also fans of the graphic novels either dismissing phoenixstorm because she has only watched the film or adding more depth to the case for either side through reference to the original material. The argument is in effect won – in 'true' fans' eyes – because of their greater knowledge and more long-standing passion for the graphic novels.

Phoenixstorm's original post attacks the perceived misogyny of the film as follows:

> I hated this movie.
>
> Yes I loved the Look of it but the script was sexist and piggish.
>
> The women were worthless and powerless whores. Yes, whores. Proud to be whores too. I guess that's every straight man's dream. Fine I could accept that all the women minus two characters were whores but then they go and make them powerless and needy.
>
> . . .
>
> All the machine guns were just window dressing. Its like some sick little boys preteen fantasy. Naked chicks and guns. How original. They weren't even meanacing. Just pathetic.
>
> . . .
>
> Then you have three strong male characters. Whatever.
>
> . . .
>
> Thanks mr. miller.

In full, the post dissects the main roles further and a lot of members respond with similar detail. The film being so faithful, characterization is fairly consistent from page to screen. It is when phoenixstorm expressly states that she hasn't read the graphic novels, however, that this becomes the main issue: 'I cant speak to the comic. I am soley gong by this movie. This movie shold be able to stand alone without an audience member having to rely on the source material' (16/4/05). Making a particular feature of being able to quote other posts, some responses follow in terms of insults. In response to phoenixstorm's comment about 'preteen fantasy', for example, {(Anonymous)} replies: 'welcome to comics . . . and stop *****ing, its just a movie' (16/4/05). And in reply to her comment, 'The last refuge of the ignorant: name calling', Rizpower replies: 'Or the lazy . . . Read the books, then come back and *****' (16/4/05).

This sense of knowledge over ignorance – the true fan versus the mere film viewer – does take over from the actual argument to a certain extent. It is an argument that is simply validated, in fact, in sexist comments and attacks on phoenixstorm, the most oddly balanced of which is from {(Anonymous)}: 'why are you wasting your time by coming to a bunch of fan boys and complaining about sexism' (16/4/05). On the whole, though, this heated thread does settle back into the main argument with reference to both the graphic novels and the film. This remains at the level of characterization to a large extent: for example, how powerful the female characters can be regarded in their hold over the damaged male characters. A number of posts, however, turn to the look of the graphic novels and film. Although providing for something of a stylistic excuse, it is nevertheless entirely appropriate with regard to the fact that the graphic novels were influenced by film noir. As skruloos, for example, states:

> Sin City is obviously not trying to be a moral representation of what the world should be. It's a celebration of a genre, one that happens to be steeped in sexist ideology. Why should Miller dilute his vision to please some kind of moral group?

> Let's face it. Noirs are sexist. There are essentially two type of women in conventional noirs: the dame in distress and the femme fatale. But the men don't fair much better either. There are the gangsters, the corrupt cops, the innocent pawns, or the hardboiled guy with delusions of chivalry. These are the kinds of archetypes that inhabit that Noir world that Sin City so brazenly celebrates. (17/4/05)

Whatever their general limitations, large fan sites such as SHH still provide an organic community. Going in to try to prove a particular argument relating to online fandom isn't necessarily the point. Rather, the analysis must be open to the live nature of the internet and the chosen communities within that.

5 Films and videogames

Videogames have been studied in a variety of ways for over thirty years, in terms of: behavioural effects and cultural impact; 'virtual worlds'; the historical and commercial development of videogames; and comparisons and contrasts with existing forms such as literature and cinema (see Smith 2002; Wolf and Perron 2003b; Newman 2004).[1] Videogames have only recently come to be studied systematically, however, through the emergence of Game Studies. As Espen Aarseth (2001) argues, the problem with the comparative approach to videogames is that looking at them in conjunction with literature, film and the visual arts often negates the essential properties that make them, most of all, *games*. Based on the initial distinction between narratology and **ludology**, Game Studies focuses on distinct elements of design, play and players (see also Juul 2001). Although Game Studies has provided a much needed focus, other approaches have come to firm up on what it means to analyse videogames in relation to narrative-based media as well as bringing attention round to the previously neglected study of play. That is, videogames can be analysed in terms of narrative, play or both (see King and Krzywinska 2002; Frasca 2003a and 2003b).

In this chapter, I will be looking at 'films as videogames' and 'videogames as films'. Within the context of this study as a whole, my approach is necessarily comparative but I will also be highlighting the main contrasts between each of the forms. In the first section, I will be looking at films and videogames in terms of film form, narrative and aesthetics. In the second section, I will be shifting the emphasis more towards videogames in terms of spatial narrative, graphics and the use of cinematic elements to complement gameplay. My case studies will focus on the *Resident Evil* games and films, and the cinematic videogame, *Metal Gear Solid 2: Sons of Liberty*.

Films as videogames

Films come into contact and can be compared with videogames in several ways, from shared commercial strategies to direct adaptations and similar textual properties. While the shared commercial strategies can primarily be said to benefit the videogame industry using similar models of development, production and promotion, the most obvious way that it benefits the Hollywood film industry is in terms of merchandising. Figures surrounding the growth of the videogame industry have certainly benefited from comparisons with film. From 1997 to 2003, for example, the 'interactive leisure software market' in the UK grew over 100 per cent, far outstripping cinema box office (30 per cent) and VHS and DVD rental (14 per cent). The global market was worth $18.2 billion in 2003 and *Screen Digest* estimates that this will reach $21.1 billion by 2007 (ELSPA 2004). That the videogame industry is also dependent on the interplay with Hollywood, however, cannot be underestimated. Blockbuster films regularly translate to commercially successful games, with five of the top twenty selling games in the UK in 2004, for example, being directly based on films: *Spider-Man 2*, *The Incredibles*, *Harry Potter and Prisoner of Azkaban*, *Shrek 2* and *The Lord of the Rings: The Return of the King* (ELSPA 2005).

Adaptation

What have been termed 'spin-offs' or 'tie-ins' present us with the first level of films as videogames, that of adaptation. As Marsha Kinder argues, while film adaptations of games generally remain unsatisfactory,

> Game adaptations of films have fared somewhat better because they usually have richer characters and more elaborate narratives to draw on, especially in works such as *Blade Runner* and *Star Wars* that inaugurated paradigmatic shifts in visual culture, which can be enhanced by kinetic action and new modes of identification. (Kinder 2002: 119)

To value narrative, as Kinder does, is to evoke an initial divide between films and videogames, the 'sketchy' characters and narrative 'shell' of popular games as opposed to the 'richer' characters and more 'elaborate' narratives of (popular) source films. The benefit of videogame adaptations of films is here regarded in terms of 'kinetic action' and 'new modes of identification', both of which are important in terms of play but the former relating to action and the latter broached more in terms of association. In videogame publishing, the success of games based on films is, first and foremost, their success as games. 'Graphics' and 'sound' are important review categories in terms of the look and feel of given games – in themselves and in their likeness to source films – but 'gameplay' and 'difficulty' are the overriding categories. It is in this respect that while such adaptations tend to score higher in terms of graphics and sound, they fall short with regard to originality of gameplay and very few are included in critical videogame polls. Only two featured in *Edge* magazine's millennial survey, 'The 100 best games of all time': the game they consider the best of the *Star Wars* licence, *X-Wing versus TIE Fighter* (1997) at number 39, and what many have regarded as the most successful film tie-in, *GoldenEye* (1997) at number 3 (Edge 2000). Similarly, Gamespot's Top Rated included only three film-related titles for the entirety of videogame releases from May 2003 to May 2004, *Star Wars: Knights of the Old Republic*, *James Bond 007: Everything or Nothing* and *The Return of the King*. On the whole, game adaptations of films are regarded as primarily commercial enterprises and remain too faithful to cinema to expand the horizons of gaming.[2]

Narrative and spectacle

Looking more specifically at films likened to videogames, there are first of all those that make thematic use of videogames; that is, films in which characters actually play games or become involved in VR game worlds. This is a distinction that takes us from films such as *War Games* and *The Last Starfighter* to *eXistenZ* (1999) and *Spy Kids 3-D: Game Over* (2003), falling short of more extensive cyberspatial films such as *Johnny Mnemonic* (1995) and *The Matrix* (see Newman 1999; King 2000: 189–91; Keane 2002). The most fruitful line of enquiry into films as videogames, however, is to look at films that are constructed around some of the main principles of games in terms of narrative, form and aesthetics. The question of narrative is particularly interesting in this respect. Exactly what does it mean for a film to make use of videogame narrative? In his stripped-down analysis of Luc Besson's *The Fifth Element* (1997), Warren

Buckland looks at the ways in which the film 'combines traditional narrative structures (the psychologically-motivated cause–effect narrative logic) with a logic based on video game rules'. As Buckland states:

> These rules, which are reliable in that they are systematic and unambiguous (for they are unencumbered by morality or compassion), constitute the video game's environment, or location, which is not restrained by the laws of the physical world. The game user can experience video pleasure primarily by attempting to master these rules, that is, decipher the game's logic. (Buckland 2000: 159–60)

Buckland provides us with a definition of game rules that is much more systematic than film narrative, a stronger logical drive that has to remain so in order for games to work. He then isolates some of the most common videogame rules: serialized repetition of actions; multiple levels of adventure; space-time warps; magical transformations and disguises; immediate rewards and punishment; pace; and interactivity. Based around a quest narrative taking part in various locations as the hero attempts to unite the fifth element with the four existing elements, Besson's film comprises all of the above except for interactivity. Even where *The Fifth Element* does make use of videogame visuals in its special effects, the film is too much representation to allow for true interactivity. In short, it's a film and not an actual videogame.

Combined with consideration of narrative, aesthetic comparisons between films and videogames bring us back round to the spectacle-versus-narrative argument outlined in Chapter 3. Blockbusters are often likened to videogames as a convenient shorthand for the waning of narrative and their principal focus, instead, on action and spectacle. Digital special effects have been said to make contemporary blockbusters even more like videogames and, aimed at a shared youth market, have come to communicate through a combination of, first, MTV and, now, videogame aesthetics. Of all the films likened to videogames, two have garnered particular attention and criticism, *The Phantom Menace* and *Pearl Harbor* (2001). Videogame-style sequences within films have been identified in terms of aesthetics, speed and perspective. We can look at a film such as *The Phantom Menace* in terms of the whole and with regard to its most game-like sequence, the pod-race. As Geoff King and Tanya Krzywinska state:

The pod-race offers a combination of views of the action. First-person shots, in which we appear to take on the perspective of Anakin, are inter-cut with a range of other viewpoints: apparently neutral 'objective' shots and those approximate to the perspectives of spectators, including the other principal characters. Similar perspectives are offered when this kind of race or pursuit action is provided by computer games, which commonly offer the player a choice of first or third person vantage points . . . The kinds of movements that are involved – high speed ducking and weaving around the alarming contours of the racetrack – are also the familiar stuff of computer games, and of film-based rides. (King and Krzywinska 2000: 100)

Where most of the other action elements in the film were covered in the *Star Wars Episode I: The Phantom Menace* game, the pod-race resulted in its own videogame, *Star Wars Episode I: Racer*. A game-like sequence in the film easily adapted into a videogame might lead us to ask which came first, but this is too literal a reading of the fluid convergence at work here – the film selling the game and the game selling the film. And taken as a sequence adapted into a whole game, the narrative element in this adaptation is virtually absent whereas the pod-race sequence can be read as serving several narrative purposes within *The Phantom Menace* (see also King 2000: 184–9).

Science fiction would appear to be the film genre most open to videogame elements but they become even more of a suspicious feature in the context of the real and the historical. As film critic David Thomson argues, *Pearl Harbor* replays history as a videogame, its professed authenticity giving way to empty simula-tion. In particular, focusing on its director Michael Bay, Thomson identifies 'the essential Bay shot' as the point-of-view shot of the bomb that falls on the US Arizona: 'it has all the gravitational zest, and the denial of damage or tragedy, that's built into the trigger-jerking spasms of video games' (Thomson 2001: 35). Film reviewers, of course, spend their time watching films, not playing videogames. The comparison with videogames, therefore, is criticism conveyed through what they regard as a lesser form. As Patrick Crogan argues: 'Thomson employs a common stereotype of videogaming to condemn *Pearl Harbor*, namely, that gaming induces an uncompli-cated but addictive sensory-motor engagement that de-emphasises intellection' (Crogan 2003: 284). Using the PC game, *Combat Flight Simulator 2: WW II Pacific Theater* (2000), Crogan looks at the skills required in this real-time genre that works independently of both narrative and spectacle. He regards the main comparisons between blockbusters and videogames as being the result of cinema's increasing dependence on digital effects. If narrative falls by the wayside in and amongst all of the frenetic spectacle, then that's as much a fault of the films themselves as anything one might say about videogames.

Hybridity

The most refined comparisons between films and videogames arise out of films where the videogame elements are in effect invisible, thoroughly integrated as they are into their overall form and construction. Combining playful and conceptual narratives with the requisite visual elements, these films are essentially hybrid in nature and take us beyond the spectacle-versus-narrative argument as applied to the blockbusting interplay between films and videogames. Marsha Kinder highlights the following as 'combining the distinctive conventions and pleasures of games and movies in original ways':

- 'recent complex action films' such as *The Matrix*, *Run Lola Run* and *Crouching Tiger, Hidden Dragon* (2000)
- 'comedies and thrillers with experimental narratives' such as *Groundhog Day* (1993), *Being John Malkovich* (1999) and *Memento* (2000)
- 'demanding experimental films' such as Wim Wenders's *Until the End of the World* (1991), Peter Greenaway's *The Pillow Book* (1996) and *Timecode* (Kinder 2002: 120).

The two most common examples of this complex hybridity are *The Matrix* and *Run Lola Run*. In *The Matrix*, the videogame elements are wrapped up in the overall virtual dynamics of the film as Neo and co. essentially make use of those elements to help them through. The Construct, for example, allows practice levels that enable the characters to hone their fighting skills. There is also something of a direct interface in the film in the form of the navigator, Link. Part-hacker and part-player, Link monitors the situation on screen, guiding the player-characters through convenient routes and locating near-by exits during emergency situations. He is also able to activate 'cheats', instantly downloadable skills such as mastery of kung-fu and being able to pilot a helicopter. And all of this in the mix of game genres that the film appropriates, from *Mortal Kombat*-style martial arts to the *Doom*-style shootout in the Lobby as guards pop up from behind pillars (see Hunt 2002; Cubitt 2004; Wood 2004). With its mix of film, video, animation and music, *Run Lola Run* finds its videogame focus in the central narrative, played out as it is three times and progressing according to mistakes made and skills learned. The film is entirely determined by Lola. At root, she is a cross between Mario and Lara Croft, permanently running and overcoming obstacles, her whole destiny dependent upon quick decisions. The wrong choice and she will have to play the game narrative again (see Grieb 2002).

Videogames as films

In this section, I will be turning more directly towards technical elements of videogames, looking at narrative, graphics and the use of cinematic devices to complement gameplay. I will be looking at the ways in which these factors, far from being regarded as mere dressage or storytelling elements separate from gameplay, can be read in terms of 'cinematic gameplay'. The earliest approaches to narrative in videogames come to us through the basics of interactivity, that players have an active role in the game and, consequently, the unfolding story. Many of these approaches betray the disciplines from which they originate, with academics from literary, drama and film studies backgrounds looking at videogames in terms of 'interactive fiction', 'interactive theatre' and 'interactive cinema' (see, for example, Laurel 1993; Friedman 1995; Murray 1997). But these approaches are also very much dependent on the games available at the time: the term 'interactive fiction' highly appropriate for early text-based computer games such as *Adventure* (1976) and *Zork* (1981), and the videogame industry then seizing upon the new opportunities afforded by CD-ROMs in being able to include Full-Motion Video (FMV) cut-scenes. Following on from the success of *Myst* (1993), these self-confessed 'interactive movies' provided the most literal combination of gameplay elements and filmic cut-scenes, from the *Wing Commander* series through to direct film and television tie-ins such as *Star Trek: Borg* (1996), *Blade Runner* (1997) and *The X-Files Game* (1998). As game designer Chris Crawford argues in relation to *Myst*, the interactive movies of the

1990s didn't so much represent the successful combination of films and games as end up a clumsy soldering job:

> While there's plenty of narrative in the game, none of it is interactive. Moreover, what interactivity there is lies far from the narrative. The puzzles that one solves in *Myst* have nothing to do with the story; it's as if two completely different media were grafted onto a single CD. (Crawford 2003: 260; see also Perron 2003)

One step on from regarding videogames as solely interactive narratives has been closer attention paid to the *spatial* properties of videogames. As Henry Jenkins argues in his particular focus on the Mario games, there are problems with the supposition 'that traditional narrative theory (be it literary or film theory) can account for our experience of Nintendo® in terms of plots and characters'. Jenkins argues that the typical Nintendo sales pitch is all about 'interactivity rather than characterization . . . and about atmospheres rather than story'. Similarly, in the games themselves:

> Nintendo®'s central feature is its constant presentation of spectacular space . . . Its landscapes dwarf characters who serve, in turn, primarily as vehicles for players to move through these remarkable places. Once immersed in playing, we don't really care whether we rescue Princess Toadstool or not; all that matters is staying alive long enough to move between levels, to see what spectacle awaits us on the next screen. (Fuller and Jenkins 1995: 60–1)

Our not caring about rescuing Princess Toadstool is a bit extreme. But 'she' is only important insofar as she represents the end of the game. As far as characterization is concerned videogames are, indeed, generally less successful than novels and films. Character development becomes a matter of the player mastering certain skills and tragic flaws are reduced to a declining energy bar. And with the tasks in each level remaining more or less the same (run, jump, shoot, find the key to the next level), the illusion of narrative progress is such that the levels merely have to look different. As Jenkins states, 'plot is transformed into a generic atmosphere – a haunted house, a subterranean cavern, a futuristic cityscape, an icy wilderness' (Fuller and Jenkins 1995: 61).

This consideration of videogames as spatial narratives is valuable in that it goes some way to addressing videogames in terms of both operation and representation. Subsequent studies have gone more into the inner workings of videogames, primarily the ways in which videogames function according to mathematical constructions that translate into essentially spatial considerations (see, in particular, Murray 1997; Manovich 2001; Ryan 2001). The resulting immersive properties cannot be developed without consideration of videogame graphics, in particular the development from 'abstraction' to 'simulation' and from 2D to fully fledged 3D environments.

Graphics

With its preference for computer rather than console games and play over narrative, graphics have received relatively little attention within Game Studies. But an understanding of graphics is absolutely essential for understanding not only representational associations between film and videogames but also gaming itself. Graphics can be approached on several levels:

- The interface, referring to the on-screen layout that not only shapes the presentation of the game but also allows the player to progress without resort to option screens;
- The spatial and immersive properties of locations and environments;
- Detail and realism, regarded in terms of the material rendering of locations and characters, and in terms of atmosphere and effects;
- Movement, understood in terms of both player-character 'moves' and smooth progress through navigable spaces; and
- Perspective, which in film terms is most commonly associated with the camera.

Computer and videogames have progressed from 'abstraction' to 'simulation' (Wolf 2003a). From the first acknowledged computer game, *Spacewar* (1962), and arcade games such as *Pong*, *Space Invaders* (1978) and *Pac-Man* (1980) through to early console games, we were basically presented with lines and sprites. Subsequent videogames have become much more representational, with developments in perspective and material rendering leading to definite characters moving through fully fledged locations rather than empty spaces. The earliest games were in 2D. Allowing for side-on or top-down views, here the pixel characters were granted freedom of movement but against essentially empty or static back-drops. Hence, games of this period tended to favour mazes and maps. This was remedied by the introduction of scrolling 2D and what has been termed 'two-and-a-half dimensional' graphics. Scrolling 2D, as evidenced in games such as *Defender* (1980) and the NES adven-tures of Mario, allowed for a much more fluid sense of movement and exploration, while 2.5D, featured in games such as *Moon Patrol* (1982) and the SNES adventures of Mario, added a sense of distance through the use of overlapping plains.

It is with the introduction and development of 3D, however, that we can now begin to talk about the more fully immersive navigation of spaces and environments. **Vector graphics** and isometric 3D are two of the earliest developments in this field. Isometric 3D, intro-duced in *Zaxxon* (1982) but still evident in games such as *Civilization* (1991), *SimCity* (1989) and *Command and Conquer* (1995), allows an angled perspective on dimensional shapes. It was principally vector graphics, however, that took hold at this time. Introduced in third-person form in *Lunar Lander* (1979) and *Asteroids* (1979), the first acknowledged first-person vector game was *Battlezone* (1980). Permitting a potentially infinite lined perspective, this 'wireframe' technique nevertheless left a lot of space to fill, and the next step was to give solidity to those blank spaces. This was first done in the move from pixels to polygons, as evidenced in the first wireframe 3D game to feature polygon-filled graphics, *I, Robot* (1983). The next devel-opment, still with us today, was **texture mapping**, essentially filling out the skeleton of lines, shapes and forms in order to give a sustained material texture to locations. *Wolfenstein 3D* (1992) is regarded as the first genuine first-person game in this respect. Where previous games had the player-character sitting in tanks and spaceships, the simple introduction of a hand at the bottom of the screen became the true marker for a first-*person* perspective and this was soon consolidated by *Doom* (1993), *Hexen* (1994), *Quake* (1996) and *Unreal* (1998). Pre-rendered backgrounds were popular in the early 1990s. In games such as *Myst*, this allowed greater detail in essentially static back-drops. But the defining mode of first-person shooters is its use of 'real-time' graphics, allowing a more fluid sense of perspectival movement through the scrolling locations (see Poole 2000: 125–48; McMahan 2003).

To distinguish between locations and environments, the former can be defined in terms of solidity and the latter in terms of atmosphere.

Characteristic videogame locations, in this respect, include the insides of buildings, tombs and so on, principally rooms and corridors. Environmental effects may well appear in these locations and outdoor environments such as mountains and forests are as much locations, but environmental effects are often much greater in wide-open spaces. The further distinction, then, is that between place and space. As Steven Poole outlines, videogame graphics come to us from numerous sources. Graphic design is key to understanding the construction of form and perspective, and art provides us with elements of contour, depth of perspective, and impressionistic light and shade (Poole 2000: 141–5). Primarily, Poole argues that graphics – and sound – are both aesthetic and functional. Enhanced solidity, in this sense, provides for a greater, material realism but a materiality that has come significantly to benefit gameplay. On one level, this refers to the fact that players are now able to interact with locations much more. But practically speaking, developments such as texture mapping and **bilinear filtering** also work in overcoming previous flaws such as the break-down in pixels when approaching objects up close or being able, literally, to run through the bodies of enemy characters. Environmental effects also have practical functions. As Poole states in relation to the *GoldenEye* game, the innovative 'distance blur' was as much to disguise the limited rendering of distance as to provide for atmosphere. But this and other effects such as lens flares and shadow have come to be used as part of the overall gameplaying experience, in effect combining the see and do of videogames as a sniper can't quite see his target, for example, or zombies suddenly appear out of the darkness.

Cinematic elements

While contributing more traditional elements to videogaming such as narrative and characterization, cinematic elements also work in terms of design, presentation, and aesthetics and function as outlined above. The most cinematic games are very much presented like films with title sequences, closing credits, 'realistic' sound effects, and an overall musical soundtrack that provides narrative- and character-based themes but is also used to punctuate the in-game action. Characters are invariably voiced by generic performers but videogames have increasingly come to make use of familiar actors, whether Michael Madsen and Michelle Rodriguez in *Driv3r* (2004) or original cast members as in EA Games' *James Bond 007: Everything or Nothing* (2004) and *The Godfather* (2006). Cut-scenes provide us with the most obviously cinematic elements of videogames, in the sense that we merely sit back and watch them, but cinematic effects have also entered into the so-called 'physics' of videogames. Two of the most recent, for example, are slow motion, as introduced in *Alien vs. Predator* (1999), and motion blur, as evidenced in the flo-motion effects of *Max Payne* (2001) and the *Matrix* games (see Edge 2004). But the most important cinematic element used in videogames is the camera. This refers not only to obviously cinematic games but also videogames in general.

As Mark J.P. Wolf (2001c and 2001d) argues, videogames rely upon a much more coherent sense of space and a much more cohesive sense of time than film. Videogame spaces have to be consistent for players to make their way through respective levels; and although games may well adopt camera angles, the real-time rendering and flow are such that games provide continuous takes without resorting to edits. As Steven Poole states, while the film camera both records and creates what we see onscreen, the videogame camera is entirely devoted to the creation of spaces that don't actually exist. Providing a visual frame, to regard it as a camera is to fundamentally help the illusion that what we are participating in is actually happening (Poole 2000: 91). Videogame cameras have come to work through a variety of perspectives. The third-person perspective brings us closest to comparisons with film. While the first-person perspective shares similarities with 'subjective' or point-of-view shots within film, it has been regarded as much more psychologically immersive in that the player effectively becomes the character. Many games, however, offer a degree of choice. Third-person games regularly feature the choice of first-person, especially when it comes to stealth and shooting. This may be voluntary or automatic, the player choosing to use a sniper rifle, for example, or the instant result of being trapped in a confined space. What they lose in terms of identification, third-person games provide the most versatile angles and perspectives, following at distance enough for the player to see the whole of the character and also providing as wide and functional perspectives as possible.

In the following case studies, I will be following 'videogames as films' through to: the *Resident Evil* games and films; and *Metal Gear Solid 2: Sons of Liberty*. The *Resident Evil* games have been influenced by horror films in several ways. How do they combine cinematic elements with gameplay? And what happens when the games are adapted into films, as in the first *Resident Evil* (2002)? The *Metal Gear Solid* games have also been regarded as cinematic. Is this just a case of sitting back and watching cinematic cut-scenes or is there more to the games in terms of cinematic gameplay?

Case study 7

ADAPTING *RESIDENT EVIL*

Like comic books, videogames provide a continual source of adaptation. Videogames first came to be adapted into film in the early- to mid-1990s with films such as *Super Mario Brothers* (1993), *Street Fighter* (1994) and *Mortal Kombat* (1995). The current wave has included *Final Fantasy, Lara Croft: Tomb Raider* (2001), *Lara Croft – Tomb Raider: Cradle of Life* (2003), *Resident Evil, Resident Evil: Apocalypse* (2004), *Doom* (2005), and based on the comics and the games, *Alien vs. Predator* (2004). Film adaptations of videogames have generally proven unsuccessful in both critical and commercial terms. The most successful have achieved only moderate domestic box office, with *Tomb Raider* at $130 million, *Mortal Kombat* at $70 million and the two *Resident Evil* films at a combined $90 million. *Super Mario* and *Final Fantasy* proved expensive failures at $21 million and $32 million respectively. As Ben Fritz and Dave McNary state, Hollywood has come to adapt videogames based on a false assumption, that popular videogame licences will naturally translate into popular films. The lesson learned from comic book adaptations, however, is that 'it's not the popularity of the license that matters so much as the foundation it provides for compelling characters, conflicts and visuals' (Fritz and McNary 2004: 2). Where planned adaptations such as *Hitman* and *Max Payne* may well come to provide for mere action movies, writer Alex Garland is currently working on adapting *Halo* and videogame auteur Hideo Kojima is closely involved with the proposed film version of *Metal Gear Solid* (see Schwarzacher 2004; Brodesser and Fritz 2005).

What is particularly noticeable about current adaptations is that, unlike the platform and beat-'em-up derived *Super Mario* and *Street Fighter*, for example, they have come to be based on games that can already be said to be influenced by cinema. The *Resident Evil* games were amongst the first to be claimed as cinematic. Ostensibly based on aspects of George Romero's *Living Dead* (1968–85) trilogy, first of all the games can be approached in terms of genre. What needs to be borne in mind about videogame genres is that they are also defined by particular modes of action. While the *Resident Evil* games can well be likened to horror films, they belong to the 'survival horror' genre of videogames, which relies upon mastering skills in order to avoid zombies as much as confronting them head on. This is implicit in all zombie horror films but where our desire to see confrontation and death is often fed by a range of characters whittled down throughout the course of a film, here the focus is on one or possibly two game characters and when they die that is the end of the game. So, where 'horror' provides what might be termed the aesthetics of these games, 'survival' refers to the type of skills required. Mastering survival also ensures longevity of play, beyond the ninety minutes or so of horror films.

Alone in the Dark (1992) is generally acknowledged as the first survival horror game. Becoming an eventual trilogy on the PC, the games made a virtue out of their relatively limited graphics, the darkness providing atmospheric compensation for the point-and-click action. Where Konami's *Silent Hill* series (1999–) provides more character and diversity, Capcom's *Resident Evil* games remain the most consistent and popular of the genre. The series has played out across numerous consoles, beginning with *Resident Evil* (1996), *Resident Evil 2* (1997) and *Resident Evil 3: Nemesis* (1999) on the PlayStation and then *Resident Evil: Code Veronica* (2000) on the Dreamcast and PlayStation 2. While the classic PlayStation-era formula has remained more or less intact, the official continuation of the series on the GameCube and PlayStation 2 in the form of *Resident Evil 0* (2002) and *Resident Evil 4* (2005) has led to greater refinement of graphics and control. Attempts to diverge from the established formula, such as the first-person *Resident Evil: Survivor* (2000) and online *Resident Evil: Outbreak* (2004), have remained little more than diversions. There is a strong commitment to narrative in the series. Founded on the release of the dreaded T-Virus in Raccoon City by the nefarious Umbrella Corporation, the narrative spreads in almost sci-fi thriller fashion along with the virus and the conspiracy behind it. The games allow players to control two characters, each of which has different capabilities that allow them to access other locations and parts of the story. This leads to recurring characters across the series such as Leon Kennedy, Claire Redfield and Jill Valentine (see Speer and O'Neill 2000).

Partly because of its involved narrative elements, the *Resident Evil* games have been regarded in terms of 'restrictive' rather than 'open' gameplay. This applies to directed locations, the basic exploration and puzzle-solving mechanics of the games, and the point-and-shoot action. Isolated from the developing narrative and action of each of the games, they do remain relatively restricted compared to recent RPGs and action-adventure games. This is partly due to their formation in the 1990s. The characteristic waiting for doors to open, for example, can be said to add to the tension of entering a new room but originally acted as loading patterns for the next location. It is in this respect that the cinematic elements of the classic-formula *Resident Evil* games have been said merely to add to the relative constrictions in gameplay. With their pre-rendered backgrounds, static third-person perspective and fixed camera angles, there is an affective claustro-phobia but also an initial sense of being completely powerless. That the games are so composed, the characters tightly framed and possible courses of action so directed has led Steven Poole to criticize such cine-matic games, making the distinction that players should benefit from being both spectator and protagonist. In horror films, often stylized camera angles are essential in constructing and developing tension:

> But in a videogame . . . this becomes a fraudulent and frustrating method of inducing tension: the player can get killed by zombies not because the environment is cleverly designed but because he or she was deliberately hindered from seeing them coming until too late . . . As with film, shots are done *to* you. (Poole 2000: 94–5)

As Tanya Krzywinska argues, however, this is exactly the main feature of survival horror games. Where horror films derive much of their power from the viewer not being able to intervene, horror games work through the dynamic of being both '*in control*' and '*out of control*'. This enables 'a *more* acute experience of losing control than that achieved by most horror films' (Krzywinska 2002: 215–17; see also Carr 2003). Regarded in these terms, the locked camera angles actually add to the expectation and anxiety, typi-cally a zombie groan heard off-screen leading the player to either shoot left and right or await their possible appearance. Both options have their disad-vantages, either wasting ammunition or waiting too long. This is also sustained in what Poole does value in terms of the overall 'tempo' of the *Resident Evil* games. Specifically, long periods of wandering around are punctuated by startling moments that are particularly unexpected in videogames, such as zombie dogs smashing through windows. Thus, the games alternate between 'suspense (not giving you what you expect, hold-ing back) and shock (giving you what you don't expect)' (Poole 2000: 200–1).

Film adaptations of videogames have the potential to open out their source material. Rather than being based on one particular game, for exam-ple, they tend to create a new story which includes various elements from the games. This is certainly the case with the first *Resident Evil* film. The film begins with an accident at the Umbrella medical facility. It then moves on to the character of Alice (Milla Jovovich) who wakes up in a bath with amnesia. Starting with a shot of her eye and then progressing on to her looking in the mirror, her psychology is very much wrapped up in the retro-spective plot; her fractured identity pieced together throughout the film in flashbacks to her role in the sabotage of the medical facility. A group of soldiers break through to the mansion and take Alice to the Hive entrance. Twenty minutes into the film she grabs one of the soldier's arms and says: 'Listen to me, I wanna know who you people are and what's going on here. Now!'. Alice and the audience are then filled in on the accident and the mission.

As Henry Jenkins (2001) states in his review of the *Final Fantasy* and *Tomb Raider* films, while the former replicates its source in terms of aesthetics, the latter is much more successful as a videogame adaptation in terms of its essentially spatial narrative construction. This is established in *Resident Evil* through the use of an electronic map that is used to outline the mission. A particular visual element repeated in *Resident Evil: Apocalypse* and *Alien vs. Predator*, this works in reflecting the use of maps in videogames and in its succinct graphic demonstration of the mission-based plot also defines narrative progress in terms of spatial orientation. At the heart of the Hive, the centre of the mission, the Red Queen uses a similar map and CCTV cameras to chart and hinder the team's goal. Once in the underground Hive, the main locations are: the Dining Room, Red Queen Chamber, Laboratory, Office, Utility Tunnel, T-Virus Lab, and then back to the Train Station. The first express videogame-style action takes place in the entrance to the Red Queen Chamber. Although not directly related to the *Resident Evil* games, here the soldiers have to negotiate a corridor protected by a grid of lethal laser beams. Open spaces such as the dining hall and adjoining storage chamber allow group action as the team is beset by zombies from all sides. Smaller locations such as the laboratory and office allow for more one-on-one confrontations.

Resident Evil diverges from the games in several ways: the emphasis on a group of characters; the singular location; the relatively high-tech rather than long abandoned nature of that location; and the inevitable compression of action and narrative elements. The film's most generic shortcomings arise out of its ostensible horror status. While the games have a 'mature' rating for over 17s, the film is severely compromised by its 'R' and 15-certificate ratings. The main problem, however, is that the film is pitched at the assumed market of the games; that is, the assumed market for most Hollywood action movies: teenagers. Director Paul W.S. Anderson has worked on several videogame adaptations. Director of *Mortal Kombat* and *Alien vs. Predator*, he was also writer and producer of *Apocalypse* and is producer of the forthcoming *Driver* (2006) and *Resident Evil: Extinction* (2007). Director of *Shopping* (1994), *Event Horizon* (1997) and *Soldier* (1998), there is a definite aesthetic in his work that can also be said to have colonized videogame adaptations. Lending a higher gloss to relatively low-budget productions, he works within the MTV aesthetic of filmmaking. Although both are aimed at the same teenage market, there are fundamental differences between MTV and videogame aesthetics. This becomes clear in *Resident Evil* in the mass attack in the dining hall. Although the film does make use of first-person shots as the soldiers sweep through the corridors, the rapid editing in this mass zombie attack works in both diminishing the potential gore and taking the film furthest from comparisons with videogames.

The *Resident Evil* games have already been noted for their restricted and effective, claustrophobic gameplay. If this applies mainly to the in-game action, the cut-scenes do contain their moments of action and spectacle but are also equally composed and, even where editing is involved, necessarily slower in terms of frame rate. The comparison between 'slow' game and 'fast' film is probably best made with the opening cut-scenes of the *Nemesis* and *Code Veronica* games, the former involving a street battle between police officers and zombies and the latter the heroine and a helicopter. Both of these are replicated in the film sequel, *Apocalypse*, but much faster in terms of editing and losing their distinction in and among the rest of the action. The first *Resident Evil* film does slow down for moments of tension, in particular during the appearance of the zombie dogs. Starting with a shot of the open kennels in the laboratory the film then borrows the accompanying sound effect from the games, the clicking of nails on the floor as one of the dogs approaches. Alice holds her gun, like the characters in the games, with both hands in full turn. We see this crosscutting between her POV, close-up shots of her face and movements, and third-person snippets of the dogs. This moment of horror, however, then becomes *explicitly* a moment of action as Alice shoots one of the dogs in low-budget bullet-time and then does a high-flying turnaround kick to the other. Ultimately signalling the start to Alice's super-mutant abilities, from hereon in she becomes more like a modern action heroine. In videogame terms, she might well represent the player who has come to master the controls. But she is not so much efficient as indestructible. The game has clearly been taken out of our hands.

Case study 8

METAL GEAR SOLID 2: SONS OF LIBERTY (2001)

Konami's *Metal Gear Solid* series has be regarded as cinematic at all levels from influences through to gameplay. Introduced in the original 1998 *Metal Gear Solid*, the two sequels, *Sons of Liberty* (2001) and *Snake Eater* (2004), have been criticized as much as they've been valued for making extensive use of cinematic elements. This becomes particularly manifest in their use of cut-scenes, providing compelling – if complex – narratives that result in players spending as much time watching as playing the games (see, for example, Kasavian 2001; games™ 2004). But as creator Hideo Kojima states, there is much more to the cinematic aspect of the games than cut-scenes:

> What I'm doing is creating a game, I'm not making a movie. To make the game more enjoyable and captivating, and to make the player feel like he's present in that setting, we need the cinematic element. There may be a misunderstanding in the game world when we say 'cinematic,' because that doesn't necessarily means showing a computer-generated movie in the middle of the action, and splitting everything up. (Quoted in Hanson 2003: 59)

The nearest comparison between *Metal Gear Solid 2* (*MGS2*) and film genres would be the action thriller. The opening titles present us with a grand introduction in this respect, the credits, including 'stars', appearing over a montage of scenes. The water-bound setting is introduced, assorted military units and hardware, the theme of genetics, and the high-tech Metal Gear Ray. And all of this to the strident military-themed score of Harry Gregson-Williams, composer of Jerry Bruckheimer productions such as *The Rock* (1996), *Armageddon* and *Enemy of the State* (1998), whose music punctuates the game as a whole. Presenting us with the feel and construction of a Hollywood action movie, in terms of videogame genres *MGS2* more correctly belongs to the 'stealth' genre of action-adventure games. Stealth games come in a variety of forms, from single-person 'spy sims' such as *GoldenEye* and the *Splinter Cell* games (2003–) to the commando-unit dynamic of the *Rainbow Six* (1998–) series. Mixing espionage with action, the political and the personal, the *MGS* games are characterized by a wider variety of gameplay elements and involved storylines but the basic principle of stealth remains: avoidance can be just as important as confrontation.

Following on from the Alaskan adventures of the original game, *MGS2* takes place on two ocean platforms, the Tanker and Plant. Upon starting the game, the player has a choice. Those who haven't played *Metal Gear Solid* are advised to go straight to the Plant and those who have, the Tanker. The opening CG sequence to the Tanker is very cinematic and cryptic, a scene-setting prelude rather than a mission briefing. The camera pans down from the top of the George Washington Bridge to the traffic below. In and amongst the rain, lightning and car lights, the camera stops on a hooded figure walking along the side of the bridge. He drops his cigarette, starts running to the edge of the bridge and suddenly becomes invisible. He jumps over the side of the bridge and the camera follows his outline in slow motion as he bungees down to the tanker below. When the figure finally lands on the deck he shakes off his stealth cloak and is revealed in a flash of light and lightning as Solid Snake, the hero of the first game. As Hideo Kojima explains in his commentary to this sequence, he is already playing with the player's expectations before the actual gameplay has even begun. Who is this figure? The fact that the figure is smoking may provide one clue and with lateral thinking, use of the stealth cloak from the first game. It is revealed to be Snake but with the narrative of the game ultimately involving cloning, the issue of identity is already put into question.[3] The same sleight of hand is followed through to the Plant level. The diver arriving at the oil platform is codenamed Snake but then on receiving his objectives is revealed to be a character codenamed Raiden. For the first-time player, this is merely the introduction of the game's main figure, Jack. For those who've played *MGS1* it is a unique twist to find that the hero has effectively been replaced by another player-character.

The argument that cut-scenes result in a fundamental narrative break in gameplay is, in part, historical. The use of live-action FMV in the early- to mid-1990s led to a noticeable separation between narrative and gameplay, the sequences using an altogether different, photographic aesthetic to the in-game graphics. Pre-rendered CG sequences went some way towards correcting this separation but in-game – or 'engine' – cut-scenes now provide a much more fluid integration of narrative and gameplay at both aesthetic and structural levels, generated as they are 'live' by the same graphics engines that power the games themselves (see Howells 2002). Cut-scenes fulfil narrative requirements in terms of back-story, characterization and the ongoing plot. The conspiracy element of *MGS2* essentially provides a mystery-style plot that works through twists, turns and eventual clarification. A number of personal stories are developed along with the political element but character interaction is principally relayed through the CODEC, the interface used by Snake to communicate with his tech buddy Octacon and the Colonel, and Raiden with his love interest, Rose. Although providing useful mission information, the combination of text and dialogue in these long conversations is much more 'intrusive' than the cut-scenes.

Cut-scenes can be defined in terms of timing, duration and function. The narrative segments in *MGS2* are the longest but are unlocked at appropriate times; after missions have been completed, for example, they also act as a rest and a reward. The more functional cut-scenes can be defined in terms of information and instruction. This becomes particularly manifest at the beginning of Snake and Raiden's respective missions. These relatively short cut-scenes work on a visual level that provides mission briefings and interactive control practice without recourse to the CODEC or options screen. The initial cut-scenes also work in introducing new locations. In the Tanker level, for example, we are first presented with a camera sweep over the decks. This is useful in that we are orientated to the new location and are able to see how many guards there are and where they're positioned. The most dynamic cut-scenes are the ones that come into play during action segments. The most successful in terms of integration, the action cut-scenes in *MGS2* effectively punctuate player involvement, providing a slighter wider perspective before pulsing back to the player-character in action. These cut-scenes are best illustrated in two sequences involving Raiden. After he has defused the bombs, a Harrier jump-jet appears. A short cut-scene signals its arrival and provides an instant opening out of the game after the confines of the interior of the Plant. Raiden has to fight the jump-jet with all weapons to hand and the punctuating cut-scenes appear when either Raiden or the jump-jet appear to get the upper hand. The second appears towards the end of the Plant level when Raiden, and Snake, are confronted by ninja soldiers. Although the player controls Raiden, the cut-scenes cut between Raiden, Snake and the soldiers, all in all providing a dynamic cinematic feel to the action (see Newman 2004: 92–100).

The visual and graphic elements of *MGS2* extend to two other cinematic areas that directly complement the in-game action. The first is realism, which I will look at in relation to the game's locations and environments. *MGS2* presents us with a clarity of design and atmosphere that also provide clarity of gameplay. The Tanker and Plant are man-made locations composed of corridors and rooms. Essentially presented in terms of solid, metallic environments, their sea location also affords weather conditions that are not merely aesthetic but are also just as functional as the interior locations. The opening cut-scene to the Tanker has already presented us with atmospheric conditions that, at this stage, we only watch. On taking control of Snake, however, the player is now *in* that environment. *MGS2* makes use of fluid third-person and the ability to switch to first-person. The first-person perspective allows Snake to look ahead and survey his surroundings in a much more direct manner than in third-person. This can be enhanced by use of binoculars, for example, and is automatically useful in the case of shooting and sniping. Such is the detail of the game, in fact, that the player can simply have a good look around and, when looking up on the decks of the Tanker, for example, raindrops appear on the camera as if in Snake's eyes. These environmental touches provide an atmospheric immersion, followed through to the interior of the Tanker, for example, when the camera mists over due to the change in conditions. But these environmental effects also have a function in terms of the actual gameplay. There are both 'negative' and 'positive' functions in this respect. While the rain and darkness give Snake a certain amount of cover on the decks, he must nevertheless stay out of light sources. But the fact that there are definite light sources to avoid also provides an advantage, the guards' torches, for example, highlighting which way they are facing. Playing as Raiden outside the Plant becomes an exercise in pure stealth in this respect as the sun beats down and sun flares occasionally obscure his vision. This high visibil-ity also applies to the interior but, even more so, with less room to manoeu-vre and guards and security cameras potentially around every corner.

The second in-game visual element that I would like to explore is the game's use of cameras in its moments of tense stealth action. These provide us with the most dynamic integration of cinematics and gameplay: the use of camera cinematic but the use of cameras from several perspec-tives a particular feature of cinematic gameplay. When Snake and Raiden are discovered, there is an immediate quickening in pace. Shooting the guard quickly enough might prevent him from communicating your where-abouts but the mission is now interrupted by the need to find a place to hide the guard's body. At first more likely than not, however, the alarm will be sounded and the player has to find a hiding place for themselves. The immediacy of gameplay in these moments is matched by a quickening of the music and a flurry of sounds. The automatic camera will continue to follow your moves but going to first-person may also be necessary to look around the room you are in and the Alert camera will have opened up in the top-right corner of the screen. This kinetic integration of cinematics and gameplay is then met by a concentrated stillness of the cinematic and a tension in the lack of active gameplay when a safe place is found. The pace drops and the activity, as such, entails staying still. This becomes particu-larly manifest when hiding in lockers. Here, the perspective is locked into confined first-person, the player only able to see through the slits of the door until the scanner downgrades from Alert to Evasion and then Caution. As the security levels drop, the music and noise are gradually reduced and, should there be a guard near the locker, there is only the sound of your own heartbeat. Looked at in this way, *MGS2* cuts through fundamental distinc-tions between passive watching and active gameplay. Rather than simply watching the cut-scenes, they are highly involved and integrated. And rather than simply shooting your way out of situations, there are times when you must simply appear not to exist.

6 Entering the matrix

The promotional campaign for the release of *The Matrix Reloaded* and *The Matrix Revolutions* provides a unique opportunity to look at the ways in which blockbusters are being marketed to new audiences. Filmed back-to-back and released in May and November 2003, the campaign for the films can be distinguished, first of all, on the grounds that it was very much a combined campaign. Allowing for a four-year build-up of expectation, the fact that one sequel was quickly followed by the other meant that promotion was maintained throughout virtually all of this self-styled 'Year of the Matrix'. The marketing and merchandising for the *Matrix* sequels followed similar lines to recent blockbuster franchises. But what distinguishes the campaign most of all is that it demonstrated particularly organized use of the new extended spaces for promotion, the core principle being that of a central narrative developed across multiple media (see Askwith 2003; Romney 2003). The two main pieces of associated merchandise in this respect were *The Animatrix*, a collection of nine animated shorts led by 'Final Flight of the Osiris', and the *Enter the Matrix* videogame. As producer Joel Silver enthusiastically states:

> This really is the first story that's being told in multiple mediums. It would be a good idea, to see 'Final Flight', to play the videogame, to watch *Reloaded*, to watch *The Animatrix*. I think if you go through that process and see all that and experience all that, I think it'll make it really a glorious experience.[1]

In this chapter, I will be presenting the combined campaign for *Reloaded* and *Revolutions* as a complete test case for where we are today with regard to film, convergence and new media. Beginning with the trilogy as a whole, I will first look at the films themselves in terms of special effects, narrative and meaning. Both the narrative and meaning of the films work through the principle of characters trapped in a virtual world, a world that we as spectators are also invited to experience. Then I will progress from the space of the films to the extended spaces of promotion. Building on existing aspects of film promotion, I will examine the ways in which we are now invited to participate in the promotional strategies and products surrounding contemporary blockbusters. I will end this chapter by focusing on *The Animatrix* and *Enter the Matrix*. How do key aspects of the trilogy's style, narrative and meaning transfer to its intertextual merchandise? Or are we merely invited to participate in associated products?

The Matrix

According to Thomas Schatz, there are three types of New Hollywood films: the calculated blockbuster, the 'sleeper' hit and the crossover independent film (Schatz 1993: 40–1). In 1999, three films very much typified these classifications: *The Phantom Menace*, *The Matrix* and *The Blair Witch Project* respectively. *The Matrix* appeared from out of almost nowhere, relatively unheralded apart from its cryptic, eye-catching trailers. Early reviewers of the film, unsure of what to make of it, fell back on the spectacle over narrative argument, albeit recognizing that the film offered a new type of spectacle. This is particularly evident in Todd McCarthy's review for *Variety*:

> It's Special Effects 10, Screenplay 0 for *The Matrix*, an eye-popping but incoherent extravaganza of morphing and superhuman martial arts. Ultra-cool visuals that truly deliver something new to the sci-fi action lexicon will make this time-jumping thriller a must-see among genre fans, especially guys in their teens and 20s. (McCarthy 1999: 1)

That assumed audience may well have simply been waiting for *The Phantom Menace* to arrive. *The Matrix* was released in April, a month before George Lucas's over-burdened prequel. Produced at a cost of $115 million, *The Phantom Menace* went on to gross $431 million at the US box office, instantly becoming the fourth highest grossing film of all time. *The Matrix* cost $63 million and, despite catching audiences unaware and being slightly hampered by its R rating, went on to garner a very respectable $171 million, the fifth highest grossing film of 1999. This does put *The Matrix*'s blockbuster status into some perspective but the figures don't always speak for themselves. Where *The Phantom Menace* offered an expectation that was always going to lead to disappointment, *The Matrix* was an intriguing proposition. And where *The Phantom Menace* could only offer a regressive story and digital effects bordering on animation, *The Matrix* combined relevant ideas with high-tech effects that appeared to take place in this world, the real world.

While *The Matrix* obviously tells a story, it is also organized around certain mythological and philosophical precepts. These meanings have been explored in a variety of ways, from the film's apparent use of Christian, Judaic and Hindu archetypes to a whole history of philosophy from Socrates to Jean Baudrillard (see Irwin 2002; Seay and Garrett 2003; Yeffeth 2003; Lawrence 2004).[2] In specific terms, *The Matrix* works through notions of reality. The narrative follows the course of mild-mannered hacker, Thomas Anderson alias Neo (Keanu Reeves). Drawn in by leather-clad Trinity (Carrie-Ann Moss) and led to the mysterious Morpheus (Lawrence Fishburne), it is revealed that the real world is actually a simulation. After taking the red pill that is offered to him, Neo is effectively woken up from his state of ignorance and can begin to fulfil his destiny as the One, the human whom it is prophesied will bring an end to the Matrix and free all humans from slavery by the Machines. *The Matrix* follows the initial development of Neo's powers in his battle against the internal keepers of the peace, the Agents, within the world of the Matrix. The first half of the film is replete with questions and running away; the second half provides active confrontation and answers.

The conceptual nature of *The Matrix* was a central feature of the film's advertizing. The teaser trailer presented a collection of striking images with no dialogue. The main theatrical trailer started with the same image, Trinity's flying rooftop leap, but then leading into characteristically cryptic dialogue from Morpheus: 'Have you ever had a dream, Neo, that you were so sure was real? What if you were unable to wake from that dream? How would you know the difference between the dream world and the real world?' This is then followed by the main question of the film and the campaign. Trinity whispers, 'The answer is out there Neo. It's the question that drives us', to which Neo responds: 'What is the Matrix?' Following the slow-motion lobby elevator explosion, the trailer then progresses to glimpses of the main set-pieces of the film: the lobby shootout, the helicopter escape from the roof of the government building, and Neo's subway showdown with Agent Smith (Hugo Weaving). These scenes are intercut with the following text: 'Forget Everything You Know / Forget Everything You've Seen / On April 2nd The Matrix Has You'. From ignorance to potential enlightenment, the trailer ends with Morpheus's line to Neo and to the audience: 'Unfortunately no one can be told what the Matrix is. You have to see it for yourself.'

The Matrix trailers present elements of narrative, spectacle, meaning and style. We are introduced to the conceptual nature of the film and invited to enter into the conceptual world realized by the film. These cryptic and immersive elements were also complemented by the film's two official websites, Warner Brothers' whatisthematrix and the more fan-related enterthematrix.com. With particular regard to special effects, the first invitation is to regard them in very much the same terms, as part of the narrative, meaning and overall vision of the film. Stylistically, the two main worlds in the film are colour-coded, the computer-generated world of the Matrix tinted green and what remains of the Real World blue. Most of the action in *The Matrix* takes place within the Matrix and the point here is that the time- and gravity-defying effects belong to fight sequences taking place in a virtual reality. Supplemented by skills downloaded into the protagonists' consciousnesses that are honed in the intermediate world of the Construct, the fight sequences are essentially battles of the mind run through digitally realized bodies. The now famous bullet-time technique is central to this conceptual use of special effects. Freezing time and bending space, the bullet-time moments represent 'mind over Matrix', the protagonists' mastery over their virtual surroundings.

As particularly manifest in the viewer's relationship to *The Matrix*, there are a number of contradictions that can be brought to bear on the film's supposed synthesis of narrative, meaning and spectacle. There is, first of all, the fact that the world of the Matrix is far more real than the Real World, a post-apocalyptic desert almost entirely composed of matte and effects work (a distinction that extends to Zion and particularly Machine City in the sequels). The action in the world of the Matrix is also by far the most dynamic.

Secondly, there is the fact that what we are watching is, after all, a film. When Neo addresses the audience at the end of *The Matrix*, it is a strikingly self-conscious moment. Supplemented by Rage Against the Machine's 'Wake up', we can now go back into the real world with a different view of reality. But it has taken innumerable special effects to point out that reality is an illusion and we probably want to return to the Matrix, unplugged but ready for more action. The first contradiction can partly be answered by the fact that it is precisely the Matrix's purpose to remain more real than real and an attractive enough proposition not to question it. The second contradiction can be answered by the film's cyberpunk sensibility. Only those alternatively adept at technology, it would appear, can truly expose the fact that corporations, politicians and the media make use of technology in order to peddle false illusions (see Cavallaro 2000; Haber 2003).

Focusing solely on *The Matrix*'s pioneering use of **bullet-time** can have the effect of isolating the specific technique from the overall effects, aesthetics and style of the film: its use of slow-motion and martial-arts inspired wire-fighting; the close-up fetishization of costumes, bodies, weaponry and mirrored surfaces; and the framing and editing of shots, inspired in equal parts by comic books and anime. But there is little doubt that bullet-time became a particular focus at the time, complemented as it was by numerous accounts of how the technique was achieved (see Kennedy 2003; Lister *et al.* 2003: 155).[3] A hinge point between the analogue and the digital, bullet-time is the result of 120 cameras taking a cascade of shots of the organized scene along a 360 degree arc. The effect is of a slight freezing of time as the character delivers a kick or dodges bullets in a full panoramic turn. Although the technique is only used, in full, in three sequences in the film, it also represents hinge points in the action and narrative. There is, first of all, Trinity's opening fight with the police officers, the 360 degree revolve and kick the first real sign that we're not in Kansas anymore. The most lavish use of the technique is the moment when Neo first achieves mind over Matrix as he dodges the Agent's bullets on the roof of the government building. The third full use of the technique is during the battle between hero and villain in Neo's subway showdown with Agent Smith.

Accounts of bullet-time and the overall spatial turn of *The Matrix* vary with regard to expansion or containment. As Yvonne Spielman (2003) argues, from morphing to bullet-time we have now entered into an era of 'elastic cinema' that moves us on from arguments surrounding spectacle versus narrative towards the spatial dynamics of science fiction cinema. While looking forward to the spatial overturning of the temporal dominant, however, Sean Cubitt argues that where there are still conventional narratives, there is still contradiction:

> The protagonist of *The Matrix* has to learn to want escape from its illusions, but as audiences, we want to remain in them. *Gladiator* offers a moral judgment on the Roman games, but we go to see it in order to witness them . . . Such diegetic worlds are self-contained and exclusive: only those who participate are inside the world. (Cubitt 2002: 28)

While this is particularly true of popular narratives that fall back on age-old notions of fate and destiny, Lisa Purse argues that *The Matrix* is actually highly inclusive in its special effects. The time-freeze aspect of bullet-time works in simultaneously increasing the 'wow factor' and allowing more prolonged observation. The spatial turn follows this through to potential immersion:

> Bullet-time is, in its very dynamics, an explicit expression of the need to see everything, to see the whole. It is an expression both of the film's mastery over the visual – its ability to *show* everything – but also the spectator's mastery of the visual – his or her ability to *see* everything . . . The ultimate mastery of the visual is not just to see all that can be seen, but to be *in* the spectacle itself. (Purse 2005: 159)

Reloaded and *Revolutions*

Where the promotion for *The Matrix* was markedly conceptual and the film itself can be said to have offered something of a new viewing experience, the selling of *Reloaded* and *Revolutions* was primarily based on narrative continuation and the promise of even more spectacular effects sequences. From sleeper hit to the realm of the calculated blockbuster, the sequels were accompanied by a mass of facts and figures relating to production and special effects. Principal photography – or 'initial capture' – for the back-to-back sequels took 17 months. Estimates on the overall cost of the two films vary between $230 million and, along with marketing and merchandising, $300 million. In contrast to the 412 effects shots in *The Matrix*, the sequels would offer some 2,500. And rather than specific bullet-time moments, entire sequences were emphasized in terms of spectacular numbers. The Burly Brawl sequence in *Reloaded*, for example, took one month to shoot and the Freeway sequence, filmed over one-and-a-half miles of purpose-built highway, took three months at an estimated cost of $40 million. Similar facts and figures also accompanied the Siege and Super Burly Brawl sequences in *Revolutions*. As Joel Silver boldly stated of the sequels' action and special effects: 'We've raised the bar so high there is no bar'.[4]

Moving beyond the relatively circumscribed spaces and philosophy of *The Matrix*, the sequels are driven by a more goal-oriented, time-dependent narrative that takes us into further places within the Matrix and introduces us to Zion and Machine City. Generically, *Reloaded* feels much more like an action movie than the first film and *Revolutions* a war movie. The sequels do work in putting further ideas into action, *Reloaded* allowing a greater insight into the internal workings of the Matrix and *Revolutions* ending in more overt religious symbolism as Neo works to defeat a now Satanic Agent Smith and sacrifice himself for the greater Good, in effect becoming 'One' with the Machines in order to save Zion. But, on the whole, the sequels were met with disappointment on narrative as much as philosophical grounds. Whereas *The Matrix* remained focused on Neo, Trinity and Morpheus throughout, the sequels necessarily add more characters but most of whom, particularly the citizens, crews and generals of Zion, remain fairly anonymous. They may well represent the greater stakes involved but outside the seductive world of the Matrix they only have survival to fall back on, and in the climactic Siege on Zion the main protagonists are fatally marginalized. The sequels are also overloaded with plot dialogue. While *The Matrix* was able to combine narrative and meaning, here the philosophical dialogue – as supremely characterized by the Architect – is dense rather than cryptic and it is principally left to mission-speak to take the characters to the next action sequence.

With particular regard to special effects, there is certainly something of an upgrade feeling to *Reloaded* and *Revolutions*. As Paul Willeman argues, the term 'bullet-time' was used so much around the time of *The Matrix* that it became like an advertizing slogan. Used even more as part of the promotional draw for the sequels, Willeman regards the films' insistence on 'the swivel' as being the visual equivalent of political 'spin':

With one difference, however: whereas spin implies a suggestion of fraudulent self-promotion, the visual spin appears to be something sexy and desirable, a positive salespoint bespeaking a trendy up-to-dateness. The visual spin disguises self-promotion into a 'cool' display of power. (Willemen 2004: 11)

Wrestling power from the author–narrator, digital labourers finally announce themselves gods of the machine, their new technologies foregrounded in such a way as to mark the obsolescence of mechanical filmmaking processes. The results of these huge teams working on expensive software packages are subsequently made highly visible, up there on the big screen: 'The effects then turn into an ode about its competitive advantage over film industries not (yet) capable of doing *that*' (Willeman 2004: 12).

The principal development of the sequels was in their use of **virtual cinematography**. Where bullet-time sufficed for breakthrough moments of mind over Matrix in the first film, virtual cinematography is an overall technique that provides a totalizing effect. Expanding on the digital elements used to supplement the bullet-time technique in *The Matrix*, it permits the complete flow of the virtual camera within entirely virtual sets (see Silberman 2003; North 2005).[5] Announcing itself in *Reloaded*'s Burly Brawl sequence, the total effect is dynamic and immersive. While there are times when we can see the join between the live and the virtual (the result of Neo *becoming* digital?), the sequence follows Neo from every possible swerve and angle in a series of long fluid takes as he fights a hundred Agents Smith. Used more pervasively in the Freeway chase, the world of the Matrix becomes a free-form arena in which the characters no longer need to think action, they simply act. Those missing the particularity of the bullet-time effect are also missing the point here in that the camera has effectively been freed from its arc. Neo now has superhuman abilities and can do much more than dodge bullets and grapple with single enemies.

While there is a notable disparity between *Reloaded*'s plot-laden exposition and spectacular set-pieces, and *Revolutions* simply rounds off the saga in a more conventional way than expected, we might well ask where the trilogy could have possibly gone after *The Matrix*. Rather than reducing the Matrix-versus-Reality philosophy of the first film, the sequels effectively move on from its circumscribed limits, the basic questions having already been answered. The sequels instead become a dialogue on Predetermination and Free Will, and zip in and out of the Human and Machine worlds – and the spaces in-between – with complexity among the confusion. With particular regard to narrative and spectacle, however, certain set-pieces do merely exist for themselves. Apart from introducing the now fractured Agent Smith, for example, the Burly Brawl remains a self-revolving technical exercise, its other function (the introduction of Neo's newfound superpowers) wrapped up in its own contradiction: if Neo can fly then why didn't he simply fly away sooner? The Super Burly Brawl is effectively a rematch and while the Freeway sequence successfully reinvents the action movie staple of chase sequences, it is followed by the fragmented and talkative 'end' to *Reloaded*. It is a measure of all these spectacular set-pieces taking place within the Matrix, in fact, that the Siege on Zion represents a very familiar and uninvolving sort of science fiction warfare. Ultimately, the sequels work in wrapping things up. Moving on from the philosophical essay of the first film, the three separate worlds of mind, body and soul – as represented by the Matrix, the Real World and Zion – end up united. The trilogy concludes with light pouring through the grids of the Matrix and the sun in the sky. In the end, the *Matrix* trilogy is humanist and it's taken a lot of technology to get us there.

From promotion to participation

Film campaigns can be approached in a variety of ways, very much depending on the type of film and the subsequent nature and scope of the campaign. In this section, I will begin with pre-existing, material methods of promotion and progress to the ways in which we are now, in effect, invited to participate in the new promotional activities surrounding blockbuster releases. These can then be applied to the campaign and products surrounding the release of the *Matrix* sequels. To distinguish, first of all, between marketing and merchandising: writing in relation to a time when such distinctions were possible, Thomas Schatz isolates the 'internal' and 'external' factors that contributed to the unprecedented commercial success of *Jaws* and the consequent blockbusting turn of New Hollywood Cinema (see also Gomery 2003; Lewis 2003). He isolates two particular strategies emanating from within. The first, 'front-loading', refers to maximum exposure in the run-up to the release of films. Benefiting from its own summer setting and situation, *Jaws* also helped to validate the 'Summer hit'. The external factors identified by Schatz very much came to fruition in the 1980s. These include merchandising, the advent of multiplex cinemas, and three key developments in the link between cinema and television: the use of television for advertizing and extending the afterlife of films through cable and video. This extension and recasting of Hollywood business around previously external agencies of promotion and consumption would come to have a fundamental effect on the actual films produced. Reduced to the level of the high-concept sales pitch and given all the frenetic gloss of music videos and television commercials, Schatz comments on the ways in which film narrative was now becoming more a matter of cross-referencing:

> On the one hand, the seemingly infinite capacity for multimedia reiteration of a movie hit redefines textual boundaries, creates a dynamic commercial intertext that is more process than product, and involves the audience(s) in the creative process – not only as multimarket consumers but also as mediators in the play of narrative signification. On the other hand, the actual movie 'itself,' if indeed it can be isolated and understood as such . . . often has been reduced and stylized to a point where, for some observers, it scarcely even qualifies as a narrative. (Schatz 1993: 33)

Schatz's use of the term, 'commercial intertext', is taken from Eileen R. Meehan's (1991) study of the strategies used to promote the 1989 blockbuster, *Batman*. Looking more into the actual campaign and merchandising, Meehan looks at the efficient mesh of vertical and horizontal business practices. From the vertical, Meehan isolates Warner Brothers' ownership of DC and the Warner music label, allowing them to renew interest in the Batman comics and release two soundtracks, including the best-selling Prince album. Far from relying on nostalgia and fandom, both these and external licensing agreements were designed to create a perpetual present and a ubiquitous presence, in this, the mass-manufactured and multimediated 'Year of the Bat'. Centred around the yellow-on-black Bat logo, the selling of *Batman* ensured a web of activities, coverage and products, an all-round intertext which, ostensibly emanating from the actual film text, would at all points refer to the presence of the film.

Case studies such as *Jaws* and *Batman* provide an insight into some of the material processes at work in the release and promotion of films. But what about the digital and the convergent? As Simone Murray (2003) argues, 'content streaming' is anchored in the 'emotional' properties of brand loyalty (see Introduction). This sense of emotional investment and of a consequent longevity – following the content wherever and whenever it may appear – is very much supplemented by the participatory nature of new media. As P. David Marshall (2002) argues in his analysis of 'the new intertextual commodity', this participation is primarily organized around the principles of interactivity and play. Using *Lara Croft: Tomb Raider* as one of his main examples, Marshall moves on from the natural 'event-effect' of blockbusters to what he calls the 'multimedia event'. He cites four main developments in the extra- and intertextual associations between film and new media: promotional use of the internet; videogames; the proliferation of toys and collectors' items advertized on official film websites; and the availability of information about the making of films from television promos to DVDs. The sheer amount of information, outlets and products essentially turns film promotion into a form of activity and pleasure in itself. As Marshall argues, while we can trace the new intertextual commodity to the merchandising associated with children's television shows such as *Teenage Mutant Ninja Turtles* and *Pokemon*, elements of play – of engagement, agency and performance – have become increasingly apparent in new media-based adult entertainment culture.

Having established some of the key principles relating to the release and current promotion of films, we can now start to apply these to the marketing and merchandising of *Reloaded* and *Revolutions*. Based on information gathered from the news pages of whatisthematrix.com, the timeline for the 2003 campaign was as follows:

26 January   International trailer for *Reloaded* and *Revolutions* premiered during the Super Bowl to an estimated global audience of 800 million; trailer also made available online

4 February   Press screening of 'Final Flight of the Osiris'; hands-on demo of *Enter the Matrix* also made available and launch of companion website to the

	game, enterthematrixgame.com; the first episode of *The Animatrix*, 'Second Renaissance Part 1', available for download
February–May	Further episodes of *The Animatrix* available for download
21 March	'Final Flight of the Osiris' shown in cinemas before the film, *Dreamcatcher*
10 April	Theatrical trailer for *Reloaded* released simultaneously online and through television and cinemas; 1.5 million downloads in first four days
April–May	*Reloaded* featured on the covers of a wide range of film and entertainment magazines, including *Empire*, *Entertainment Weekly*, *Premiere*, *SFX*, *Starlog* and *Wired*
15 May	World premiere of *Reloaded* and *Enter the Matrix* released
3 June	*The Animatrix* available on DVD
June–October	The IMAX version of *Reloaded* toured across the world
20 August	Teaser trailer for *Revolutions* available online
26 September	Theatrical trailer for *Revolutions* released simultaneously online and through television and cinemas
10 October	*Reloaded* available on DVD
19 October	Release of *The Matrix Comics: Volume One*
5 November	Global premiere of *Revolutions*

Beginning first with the release of the films, there have been three main developments since those identified by Thomas Schatz. With regard to front-loading, current films are caught between the slow trickle (teaser trailers released up to a year before the actual release and unbounded pre-release speculation on the internet) and the concentrated flurry, with traditional focus on the opening week having now given way to the opening weekend. Given greater exposure across a wide range of media, this is part organization but also pre-emptive, in that the more outlets there are, the more chance there is of negative reviews affecting the week's takings. This has also had an effect on the summer release schedule. Still primetime for blockbuster releases, the flipside is that there is also much more competition for individual films released over the summer period. This has eased somewhat in recent years with films such as *Lord of the Rings* and *Harry Potter* having benefited by shifting emphasis towards Christmas. *Reloaded* was released in the early summer and *Revolutions* in the pre-Christmas season. The third development has been that of world and global premieres, the former leading with a US release and the latter much more in sync with the rest of the world. Adding an international perspective to the release of films, the main benefit is that of a greater event-effect arising from global media coverage. Leading with the widest print run in cinema history, *Reloaded* grossed $91 million in its opening weekend and $281 million by the end of its domestic run. *Revolutions* grossed $48 million in its opening weekend and $139 million in total. The relatively disappointing box office for *Revolutions* can be attributed to several factors: its out-of-season November release, the campaign's primary emphasis on the first of the two sequels, and what many had come to regard as the downward turn of the saga.

The campaign made use of familiar promotional outlets such as magazines and television, and as well as high-tech merchandising there were also action figures, soundtrack CDs, 'making of' books, posters, t-shirts, collectible film cells and *Matrix*-style sunglasses. The comics were very much the first step towards a wider, intertextual universe, having been available on whatisthematrix.com since the first film. Although most apparent in *The Animatrix* and *Enter the Matrix*, the new commercial intertextuality of the sequels was most curiously evident in licensed advertizing. Five commercials were shown on television and in cinemas to accompany the release of *Reloaded*. While this strategy isn't new, and the advertisements for Powerade and Heineken aren't wholly relevant to the current argument, such commercials work in simultaneously promoting the films and the products. What is distinct about the licensed commercials accompanying *Reloaded*, however, is that they are said to go beyond mere product placement, for example, and reflect the 'mentality' of the *Matrix* films. The commercials were directed by James McTiegue, first assistant director on the sequels, and utilized some of the same crew and virtual sets. As McTiegue states: 'Anything that was going to happen with the commercials was going to have be specific to the world of the *Matrix*'.[6] It is in this respect that the three commercials promoting Samsung's 'DIGITall' range also work in replicating the look and feel of the *Matrix* films. The first of these was for the Samsung Matrix Phone, specifically designed for the sequels and subsequently manufactured for retail. The other commercials were for Samsung's V200 rotating camera phone and their latest 40-inch flat panel LCD televisions with digital picture enhancement. Both of these are narrated in terms of a 'new reality', a new reality manifest in their ability to show spectacular images and clips from *Reloaded*.

Subsequent products in the commercial and intertextual afterlife of the *Matrix* trilogy have included: the *Revolutions* DVD (April 2004); *The Matrix Comics: Volume Two* (December 2004); the 10-disc *Ultimate Matrix Collection* DVD (December 2004); and the *Matrix: Online* (April 2005) and *Matrix: Path of Neo* (November 2005) videogames. Along with its 'pioneering' computer-display website – which can usefully be read in relation to the *Blair Witch* and *Star Wars* sites from the same year – *The Matrix* DVD has also been regarded as a formative example of a new medium. Released in November 1999, several months before the equally proficient *Blair Witch* and *Phantom Menace* DVDs, it was the first million-selling DVD in Britain. As Michelle Pierson argues, this wasn't only due to the actual film:

> The DVD release of *The Matrix* will be remembered as having integrated the pleasures of going behind the scenes to explore the ideas and techniques of visual effects production into the home viewing experience more fully than had previously been attempted in this format. (Pierson 2002: 165)

While the sort of special features evidenced in *The Matrix* DVD have now become standard, Pierson isolates the link to the essay browser section of the official website and the 'Follow the White Rabbit' feature as being particularly valuable in accessing technical and broader, cultural information about the film. In relative terms, the 2-disc *Reloaded* and *Revolutions* DVDs offer little more than the now common making-of documentaries and extending to promotional features on *The Animatrix* and *Enter the Matrix*. On one level, *The Ultimate Matrix Collection* merely follows that through to the current 'box set' mentality of offering all of the previous DVDs with new material. But this 10-disc set can be regarded as particular to the *Matrix* saga in that it is also about information overload – promising die-hard fans 'ultimate' knowledge all in one package. The documentaries and features can be categorized in terms of: the transcultural influences upon, and impact of the trilogy; technical matters relating to production and special effects; and the philosophical dimensions of the saga. The latter includes a definitive documentary, *Return to Source: Philosophy and The Matrix*, and an audio commentary on each of the films by philosophers Cornel West and Ken Wilber. What is particularly noticeable about all of the above features is that they principally relate to the spectacle and meaning of the films. While obviously more promotional in nature, narrative is more a feature of the *Animatrix* and *Enter the Matrix* discs than it is of the actual film discs.

The Animatrix

Ranging from traditional anime to fully fledged CGA, the nine short films in *The Animatrix* offer a range of animation styles by different artists, writers, directors and studios. What unites these films alongside aesthetic variations on the Matrix concept is the fact that they intersect with the films and each other in specific narrative and thematic terms. The shorts that intersect most directly with the films are:

- 'The Second Renaissance' Parts I and II, which give a history of the formation of Zion and the Matrix;
- 'A Detective Story', which features Trinity and combines the initial film noir setting of *The Matrix* with its Alice in Wonderland theme;
- 'Kid's Story', which introduces the Kid who worships Neo in *Reloaded* and plays a significant part in the Siege in *Revolutions*; and
- 'Final Flight of the Osiris', the main entry that leads directly to the events in *Enter the Matrix* and then *Reloaded*.

The other four shorts take place independently of the characters and main events of the films but remain grounded in the different worlds developed throughout the trilogy: the Real World ('Matriculated'), the Construct ('Program') and the Matrix ('World Record' and 'Beyond') (see Wood 2005).

With particular regard to the aesthetic range of the *Animatrix* shorts, here I will be comparing and contrasting the most traditional of the contributions, 'Program', with the only one that makes full use of photorealistic CG animation, 'Final Flight of the Osiris'. Written and directed by Yoshiaki Kawajiri, and produced by Tokyo-based Madhouse Studios, 'Program' taps into the defining low-budget characteristics of Japanese anime. Beginning with comic strips and television series, these revolve around either slowing the action down or speeding it up in order to make dynamic use of fewer drawings. Such techniques include: 'limited motion' where the camera pans over a pre-rendered drawing; 'vacuum space' which can be used to establish settings or provide a meaningful pause in the action; slow-motion, freeze-frames and use of slide drawings; repeating the same images and character movements; and using flashes of colour, extreme close-ups, quick cutting and zooms. In effect such techniques make the editing and camera do all the work and in this respect it's easy to see why anime has gone on to influence contemporary Hollywood cinema in the way that it has.[7]

Belonging firmly to the historical as opposed to futuristic strain of anime films, as evidenced in the director's medieval epic, *Ninja Scroll* (1995), 'Program' begins with a battle between soldiers on horseback rushing towards a lone samurai girl. The 2D is made to look 3D through the use of perspective. We are presented with several receding planes throughout the film, the opening field of reeds, a bamboo forest, arches, sliding doors and rooftop peaks. In order to extend that perspective further, the backgrounds, such as the dark sky and snow-covered mountains, are mono-coloured. These give the impression of essentially flat characters existing in three-dimensional space, and put the primary colours, particularly blood, fire and the red sky, into greater relief. The use of red throughout 'Program' is significant in that the central characters have taken the red pill and this *Matrix*-informed colour-coding also extends to the soldiers breaking up into green lines of code when they are killed. The girl is revealed to be a character named Cis who is participating in her 'favourite simulation'. A male character, Duo, also enters the program and yet, like the character of Cypher in *The Matrix*, wishes that he hadn't taken the red pill and wants to regress back to his previous state of ignorance. The simulation then becomes far too real as Cis refuses to join him, she is locked in the program, and Duo is willing to fight her to the death.

In terms of bullet-time, 'Program' uses the full technique only once. 'It's ironic that one can be more at peace in the virtual world', states Duo as Cis jumps up in slow-motion. Accompanied by a 360-degree turn enhanced by the surrounding bamboo shoots, she then perches on the end of his sword. This is the most specific homage to the technique throughout *The Animatrix*. Subsequently broken down into its constituent parts, the fighting is often presented in slow-motion, at one point the camera speeds towards Cis over a slated roof, and the final breakthrough is Cis managing to slow down Duo's descending sword, catch it, snap it and stab him. Here, the technique directly relates to the narrative because she has successfully completed the test.

Written by the Wachowski Brothers, directed by Andy Jones and produced by Square USA, 'Final Flight of the Osiris' is the most Western of the *Animatrix* shorts and the one most specific to the narrative and style of the *Matrix* films. The action progresses from the Construct to the Real World and then the Matrix, crucially allowing the central character Jue to place a message in the drop point communicating the fact that the machines are burrowing their way through to Zion. Opening in a temple within the Construct, we are faced with light and space. Similar to 'Program', Jue is sparring with a man, Thaddeus, but far from going out of control the sequence becomes a seductive swordfight as the characters gradually snip away at each other's clothes. In effect, there are three levels of spectacle at work here: the pristine CGA, given detail and fluidity through the lighting and camera movements; the sight of the digitally rendered bodies in graceful and acrobatic motion, enhanced through slow-motion and, again, the flow of the camera; and both of these factors as applied through to the aesthetic nature of the bodies in what ultimately boils down to a curious striptease. Contrasted with the epic, classical charge that opens 'Program', we are provided with a mellow electronic soundtrack that makes use of choral voice and regular beats that join with the hum of the swords. The camera starts from a vertical position and then swoops down to accompany the action. Not as direct as 'Program' in its 360-degree swirl around Cis in the bamboo forest; the camera nevertheless becomes like a third partner in this sparring, seductive dance sequence, taking time out to follow Jue and Thaddeus as they jump, parry and somersault in slow motion.

Animated by the same team who made *Final Fantasy: The Spirits Within*, 'Final Flight' provides a further development of the photorealistic CGA from two years earlier. Perfecting hair and skin texture, facial expressions and physical movement, the striptease element of the sequence is curious in that it works in first announcing and then essentially hiding the fact that what we are seeing are computer-generated bodies: which is to say that they are beautiful but also in many ways *too* perfect. Then the scene suddenly shifts as an alarm leads to Jue and Thaddeus being unplugged from the training program. From light to darkness and the open space of the temple to their claustrophobic ship, the characters become locked into tight camera shots and rapid editing. 'Final Flight' then becomes a race against time as the Osiris is chased by Sentinels after the discovery of the tunnelling machines. Most clearly echoing the scenes involving the Nebuchadnezzar in *The Matrix*, rather than seeing athletic mind-bodies in action, here we see the characters confined in a metallic environment. This is given further solidity through the sounds of feet on metal, the clatter of guns and the force of the engines. The closing third of 'Final Flight', however, works in combining the two spheres of action as it cuts between the crew of the Osiris and Jue racing through the Matrix to deliver their findings to a designated drop point. 'Fly baby fly', whispers Thaddeus as Jue jacks in, smashes out of a high-rise window, leaps across the rooftops, and twists and turns through elaborate power scaffolding while falling to the streets below. Allowing for narrative development and a glimpse of the kind of advanced spectacle we go on to see in *Reloaded*, 'Final Flight' ends with direct consequences between the three main worlds in the *Matrix* saga. Although ending in defeat, the mission has succeeded and it is now the job of the videogame player to recover the information.

Enter the Matrix

Enter the Matrix opens with falling green lines of code, the characteristic computer scroll that opens each of the *Matrix* films. Accompanied by the familiar music and acting as a convenient loading pattern to the game, the invitation is fittingly solipsistic: entering into the literal cyberspace of a videogame based upon a film series which itself flits between the Real World and the computer-generated world of the Matrix. We are then presented with actual footage filmed by the Wachowski brothers on the set of the sequels. Providing the player with an hour's worth of exclusive footage is one of the main rewards of the game and the most obvious way in which it feeds into and out of the events of the film. The narrative of the game can be regarded as 'parallel' and 'intersecting' in this respect: the parallel sections alluded to in *Reloaded* but effectively taking place off-screen for players to complete; and the intersecting sections marked by using footage directly shown in the film. Internally, *Enter the Matrix* is heavily reliant on narrative elements. But this also works externally as the game ties into 'Final Flight' and both sequels. The first four chapters of the game, from The Post Office to The Airport, effectively take us out of 'Final Flight' and into *Reloaded*. The next five chapters, from The Sewers to The Power Plant, directly intersect with the events in *Reloaded*. And the final two chapters take us beyond *Reloaded* and into *Revolutions*.

The game offers two types of cut-scene: actual film footage and those generated by the game engine. Following another film sequence, the game progresses to the first game-engine cut-scene as Niobe and Ghost gather their guns in the Construct and jack in to a warehouse within the Matrix where their car awaits them. Beginning with a tidy distinction between the Real World (film footage) and the Matrix (game-engine graphics), this is quickly ignored as the game flits between film footage in and out of the Matrix, and likewise with the game-engine cut-scenes. Many of the game-engine cut-scenes, written and storyboarded by the Wachowskis, are sequences that would be welcome in the films themselves. There is, for example, Niobe somersaulting and throwing tear gas canisters back at the soldiers in The Post Office, jumping through the window, landing on a truck and diving into Ghost's car. There is also the 'boss' level at the end of The Airport when, after kicking an Agent out of the back of a plane in the gameplay itself, Niobe parachutes away. The consequence of this, however, is that the game-engine sequences are more cinematic than the film footage, which mostly deals with exposition.

With particular regard to gameplay, we are in effect playing a videogame based on a film series which itself makes use of videogame elements (see Chapter 5). *Enter the Matrix* may well be more interactive than the films but is it just as dynamic? The three main characters in the game are Niobe, Ghost and Sparks. We are given a choice between playing as Niobe or Ghost while the navigator Sparks remains our guide, accessing maps, finding exits and so on. Niobe and Ghost are principally involved in fighting and shooting, exploring and puzzle-solving, but the game also features platform elements and two other modes of play are available in terms of car sequences and piloting the Logos. Where the *Matrix* trilogy colonized all of the main staples of the action genre through its gravity-defying effects, to a certain extent the game has to bring these elements down to a controllable level. This is particularly true of the platform and car sequences. The game does, however, make use of the bullet-time effect, or as it is termed in the game, the 'Focus' move. Incorporated on both aesthetic and functional levels, the technique does at least appear to give the player-character extra time and space to battle enemies. But where the main point of the technique in the films is that we get to see movement of both camera and character, here the characters' moves are often divorced from the camera. Following the game characters from a third-person perspective (with the opportunity to click to first-person for more accurate shooting), the 360-degree turn that fully defines the effect is occasionally clumsy and fundamentally takes control away from the player as we simply watch the resulting move.

This is not to say that *Enter the Matrix* doesn't work in terms of freedom and gameplay. There are numerous levels allowing the player to explore familiar and unfamiliar locations, the choice of Niobe or Ghost leads to different progress and outcomes, the pace is such that exploration ebbs and flows with sudden riots of attack, and a 'hacking' function allows the player to activate cheats. But, the main and overriding interest is when the game directly intersects with the films. This applies not only to narrative but also the action in the game. In terms of fighting, for example, while fighting security guards, Agents and a new collection of vampires and zombies at the Merovingian's Chateau do involve the player, the real frisson comes when confronting familiar characters such as Seraph, Agent Smith and sparring partner Trinity. But this is where narrative demands manifestly override gameplay, in that these characters must remain largely undefeated for them to play their parts in the sequels. As Diane Carr argues, this is particularly evident in the Freeway and Saving Bane sequences in the game. In the former, Niobe has to get to the truck in order to save Morpheus. But, as Carr states, 'Niobe will be there on-screen, on time, in *The Matrix Reloaded*, whether the player persists or not'. And in the latter, the player has to save the character of Bane knowing full well that he will end up being possessed by Agent Smith. As Carr argues, the levels that are most independent of the films take place in something of a 'backwater', and the problem with the parallel and intersecting levels is that they are too bound to the master text (Carr 2005:

39–46). At both narrative and promotional levels, on completing the game the player is rewarded with the trailer for *Revolutions*. And, if anyone wants to watch the twenty-three film scenes without playing the game, they can simply watch Disc 4 of *The Ultimate Matrix Collection*.

We are certainly invited to watch *The Animatrix* and play *Enter the Matrix* in relation to the films, but how are we to regard the films in light of the products? Not restricted by the need to intersect directly with the sequels, *The Animatrix* is able to take time out to explore other parts of the *Matrix* universe and delve a little further into ideas surrounding reality and illusion, humanity and technology, choice and fate. Short on meaning but high on narrative and the basics of interactivity, in relative terms *Enter the Matrix* becomes a straightforward multimedia product. The 'fourth' text produced in conjunction with the back-to-back sequels and *The Animatrix*, one can certainly see the negative effects of film upon product and product upon film. Attempting to integrate gameplay with film footage, determined by the requisite narrative elements, and having to meet the film release deadline, the game ends up unfinished, not altogether accomplished and contains tell-tale coding bugs (see Gerstmann 2003). Partly due to the greater architectural demands but also learning from the rush release of *Enter the Matrix*, the makers of *The Matrix: Online* released the game a year after it was due for completion. And *The Matrix: Path of Neo* does represent something of an improvement in that, while it relives key moments from the films, it does so through levels and skills rather than linear narrative.[8] In the increasingly close intertextual association between films and new merchandising, narrative is expanded and reduced, shared and fractured. The potential effect on the master texts – the actual films – is that they also suffer, containing notable 'holes' that have to be filled by watching and playing the associated products. So, the principle of watch one, buy into them all has come to extend to issues of narrative. In the end, it is left to the true believer to get the whole picture.

Conclusion

Throughout this book we've looked at the issues, texts and activities resulting out of the recent convergence between film and new media. In this concluding chapter, I will be looking at the latest developments in terms of *transmission* and *miniaturization*. I will begin with cinema's current transition towards digital cinema and e-cinema. This will be followed by relevant developments in television and issues surrounding film content on the internet. I will then look at the latest developments in videogame consoles and the growth of micromedia. Concluding the book as a whole, the main progress is still that from big screen to small. But terms such as 'form', 'viewing', 'public' and 'private' hardly suffice when faced with the absolute flow of images and information. Forms merge, screens recede and content streams. The effects are at once fragmenting and total.

Cinema

In 2004, there was an 11 per cent increase in worldwide cinema admissions, totalling 9.6 billion visits. There were 1.54 billion admissions in the US and, at 171 million visits and a box office total of £796 million, the UK recorded its second highest figures in thirty-two years (RSU 2005). In 2005, however, US box office takings fell by 6 per cent to a total of $8.99 billion and admissions were down 8.7 per cent to 1.4 billion. Worldwide box office takings were also down 7.9 per cent to a total of $23.24 billion (MPAA 2006a). Although these figures follow on from the record-breaking totals of 2004 and worldwide box office has undergone a growth of 46 per cent since 2000, in specific terms 2005 was regarded as a disappointing year for the film industry. Several reasons have been given for the relative drop in cinema-going in 2005, ranging from under-achieving blockbusters and the ongoing rise in ticket prices to what might be considered more 'cosmetic' disadvantages, such as endless commercials and trailers before film showings, and constant chattering and mobile

phone activity when the films are being shown. What is most noticeable about current speculation, however, are the ways in which home
entertainment technologies previously regarded more in terms of
mutual advantage are now said to be having a detrimental effect on
cinema attendance. Where factors in the preference for home viewing still relate to comfort, saving money and the greater choice of
films, comfort is now a matter of the comparable big screen experience and choice also a matter of film viewing or interactivity.
Cinema-going and home entertainment, however, are not necessarily
at odds with each other. As the Motion Picture Association of
America's (MPAA) '2005 Movie Attendance Study' suggests,
cinema-goers who own or subscribe to four or more home entertainment systems such as DVD players, big screen televisions, cable,
satellite or digital television, and video-on-demand (VOD), go to the
cinema on average 8.2 times per year. In itself quite significant, those
who own fewer than four items only go 6.2 times per year. Which is
to say that those who are interested in films watch them both at home
and in cinemas. Sixty-nine per cent of the respondents also stated
their preference for going to watch films at the cinema (MPAA
2006b; see also Fritz 2005; Kilday 2006).

We have already looked at the means through which cinema has
worked in maintaining its special status as the main 'event'. From
widescreen to CGI, the next development will lie in completing the
current digital circuit of film from production to exhibition. This next
step has been given several names: 'broadband cinema', 'digital
cinema', 'electronic cinema', 'd-cinema' and 'e-cinema'. Technically
speaking, digital cinema is already with us. In 2004, there were
around 120 digital projectors in US cinemas with plans to extend that
to 2,500 by 2007. Similarly, the UK Film Council's Digital Screen
Network is planning to increase its initial 2004 figure of 18 to 250
(Silverman 2004; UK Film Council 2005). However, digital projection systems are only the first step towards fully fledged e-cinema. As
Nigel Culkin and Keith Randle (2003) explain, analogue film distribution works through the laborious and expensive transportation of
prints. This is eased somewhat in digital cinemas that make use of
DVD but the next development will be that of essentially transmitting
films into cinemas, whether through terrestrial broadband or the
current favoured method of satellite technology.

Striving to balance initial costs with long-term savings, the transition from analogue to digital exhibition is caught between various

proposed projection and delivery systems on the one hand and reluctance to implement a single, totalizing system on the other. This has been most clearly expressed by the EU. Fearing a loss of intellectual property rights, e-cinema might ultimately lead to an unprecedented rise in film piracy. And the standardization of essentially American systems could go on to undercut national film industries (see Herrold 2003). Where such debates are essentially taking place behind the scenes, digital and e-cinema are principally being promoted in terms of distribution and exhibition – promising audiences simultaneous international releases and an apparent effect on what they will experience on the big screen. Despite more sophisticated preservation techniques, analogue master prints are still prone to degradation and the quality of film showings is very much dependent on particular cinemas. From infinite source to rebooted venues, above all, digital and e-cinema promise sheer clarity of image and sound reproduction. There is a clear benefit to viewing blockbusters as we're taken even further into the spectacle and overall audio-visual experience of the films. The spectacular potential of digital cinema also looks likely to be joined by the introduction of digital 3D. Disney's *Chicken Little* (2005) was the first film to be released in digital 3D in a handful of compatible cinemas. Having already worked on the 3D IMAX documentaries, *Ghosts of the Abyss* (2003) and *Aliens of the Deep* (2004), James Cameron's first directorial feature films after *Titanic* will be the digital 3D *Avatar* (2007) and *Battle Angel* (2008). Where Cameron expects a thousand digital 3D cinemas to be ready for the former, the reception of the first film will determine not only the success of the second but also the digital 3D format in general.

Like so many developments in cinema, the emphasis is on spectacle and this is exactly part of the EU's case. Mindful of the even more dominant flow of Hollywood blockbusters, the EU and UK's plans for a 'virtual network' of digital cinemas include a certain amount of protection. In the UK, for example, 73 per cent of cinema screens were housed in multiplexes in 2004 and only 6 per cent in 'specialist' cinemas that exhibit independent, arthouse and international films. According to the Digital Screen Network, 141 digital screens will be housed in multiplex cinemas and 66 in specialist cinemas. Digital and e-cinema can also go on to be used at international film festivals and have the potential for enabling live film and multimedia events (UK Film Council 2005; see also Wasko 2002). Regarded in these terms, the distinction between independent and mainstream films will either remain or recede. Or maybe the distinction needs to remain as it can been argued that you can't have one without the other.

Television

As we saw in Chapter 1, films have found a significant afterlife in the home. Like cinema, television is an old medium that has been continually updated, whether through new modes of broadcast or various appliances such as VCRs and DVD players. These developments have come to alter previous conceptions of the passive television viewer and have also had a significant effect on film choice and viewing. Like digital cinema, but much further in its infiltration, television has fast become digital television and, now, high-definition television. Part of the international drive towards the implementation of HDTV initiated by the Telecommunications Act of 1996, digital television will result in the big 'switch off' of analogue television when digital penetration has reached over 85 per cent in respective markets. Again, image quality is a key factor in digital television. But the data compression also allows for much more choice than existing terrestrial television and an extension of the interactive features, navigable menus and 'information-rich' look of cable and satellite services. Digital television has also seen a return to widescreen film presentation and will ultimately lead to further convergence between television and the internet (see Boddy 2000; Hilmes 2002). High-definition television is the next development, in that it promises even clearer sound and vision quality. In 2006, Sky television introduced its HD service but subscribers will require not only new Sky boxes but also HD-ready television sets for the full effect.

One of the latest additional developments to television is the digital Personal Video Recorder (PVR). Partly working on the gap opened up by the clash of recordable and rewritable DVD players, and answering the problem of the great trawl required through the sheer amount of channels now available on most sets, PVRs work in storing television transmissions as data on their hard drives. The recent Sky+ system is being sold on its ability to pause and rewind live television. The 'smart' system of choice in the US, however, is TiVo. This convergent personal system offers Online Scheduling, where the recorder can be programmed remotely, and TiVoToGo which offers the ability to record or download programmes onto PCs and laptops. As well as scheduling services such as the Season Pass which automatically records each episode of a chosen series, TiVo's most notable function is that of the WishList. Part automatic in its ability to tape programmes based on viewing patterns, it can also be programmed to record programmes and films according to various categories such as genre, actor or director. Where digital television offers numerous interactive features, systems such as TiVo can be regarded as the opposite, in that they are able to do most of the work for you (see Boddy 2002 and 2003).

With particular regard to films, home cinema represents the most direct crossover of cinema and television. As Barbara Klinger states of the initial advertising of home cinema:

> Home theater advertisers have attempted to create a TV-watching elite out of the notoriously democratic television audience. The image of the couch potato, the familiar icon of the media-addicted, slothful television viewer who indiscriminately watches whatever television's flow brings his or her way, is nowhere to be found in the pages of home theater magazines . . . The ideal audience is akin to the original audiences of the Lumiere films at the moment of cinema's invention: home theater spectators react to the screen as if its images were real, testifying to this new technology's vivid powers of reproduction. (Klinger 1998: 397)

This has also been followed through to television commercials and websites emphasizing the adrenaline rush and complete control over the new apparatus of home cinema. Sharing strategies similar to the advertising of DVD (simultaneously being blown out of your seat *and* studiously clicking away at the special features), 'home cinema', 'digital clarity', 'surround sound', 'interactivity', all of these advances are contrasted with simply watching a video on a monolithic television set. Such is the ever-accelerating state of the art, however, that choice also presents consumers with dilemma. Which of the current television sets advertised on the Samsung website do you require – the LCD TV, DLP TV, Rear Projection TV, Plasma TV or SlimFit HDTV? This depends on whether you want 'clarity', 'design' or something more approaching the complete cinematic 'experience' (samsung.com). Two potential replacements for DVD are also entering into the home entertainment market: Blu-Ray discs supported by Sony, Fox and Disney; and HD-DV by Warner, Universal and Paramount. Able to hold up to six times the amount of data, these new formats look likely to replace DVD much sooner than the twenty years or so free rein granted to VHS (see Hazleton 2006).

The internet

In Chapter 4, we looked at the internet in terms of film promotion and fandom. Looking more into actual film content, first of all we might well ask: why watch films on PCs? This is very much the business of convergence, to make such formal distinctions unnecessary. The domestic nature of the internet leads to more obvious comparisons with television. As William Boddy (2000) argues, there is an essential divide between the private realm of personal computers and the domestic space of television that has led to explicitly combined PC and TV sets largely failing in their attempt to combine the two forms. But the current convergence between home computers and television isn't so much taking place between separate forms as operating at the level of *delivery*. Media companies are increasingly becoming involved in multiple delivery, or what has been termed 'quadruple play'. In the UK, for example, there is the recent example of NTL merging with Virgin Mobile. This will lead to a situation whereby consumers will be provided with landline, mobile phone, broadband internet and digital television services all from the same provider. There is a number of television services available on the internet and this looks likely to develop: from television channels available exclusively to the internet to select series and exclusive content. And some of the most recent television sets offer broadcast internet services such as those equipped with MSN TV, formerly known as WebTV.

With particular regard to film content, the direct release of films on the internet has previously taken place at the level of short films and independent feature films (see, in particular, atomfilms.com and ifilm.com). The internet has been regarded as an additional rather than primary outlet for the release of mainstream feature films and this has mainly taken place through video-on-demand. A number of sites have become involved in VOD, some originating from major studios such as Sony's MovieFly and Disney's Movies.com, and others such as World Cinema Online and ClickStar. CinemaNow is one of the most long-standing VOD sites. This can be accessed from

Warner Brothers' main site and offers 'streaming' and 'download-to-own' services mainly related to budget titles. Partly inspired by the success of online DVD rental sites such as NetFlix, Amazon and Blockbuster, however, there is currently a definite drive towards making premium films available online. With download times now reduced and the inevitable crossover between television and the internet, major studios have become very interested in VOD. In 2005, Warner began converting 5,000 films to VOD, and Sony and Universal the same with an initial amount of 500. There are also plans for MGM, Paramount, Universal and Warner to organize a site around the principles of MovieFly, and Disney and Fox in a combined effort to enhance Movies.com (see Wasko 2002; Roberts 2004).

Looking to make inroads into this new mode of distribution, the move towards VOD also represents a pre-emptive attempt by film studios to ward off the unofficial availability of films on the internet. Based on the principle of endless conversion, digital media have led to an inevitable increase in film piracy. A number of agencies and legislative acts such as the World Intellectual Property Organization and the Digital Millennium Copyright Act of 1998 have sought to protect artistic and commercial copyright in the light of digital piracy. Where analogue piracy in the form of bootleg music tapes and illegal videos has been essentially physical in nature, digital piracy is all about getting in on the flow, a simple enough transcription in the case of CDs and DVDs but far more open, invisible and difficult to police on the internet. Online piracy was first brought to the public's attention through the *Napster* case. Formed in 1999, Napster was the first widely used peer-to-peer (P2P) music file-sharing service. Napster was taken to court by leading music companies on the grounds of copyright infringement and was effectively shut down in 2001 (see Burnett and Marshall 2003; Dobie 2004; Olsen 2004). The main developments since *Napster* have been the growth of more decentralized P2P networks, cooperative subscription sites such as Napster 3.0, and official music download services such as Apple's iTunes.

Two of the major organizations involved in protecting against film piracy are the MPAA and the UK-based Federation Against Copyright Theft (FACT). The MPAA calculated that approximately $3.5 billion was lost to the US film industry in national and international revenues due to piracy in 2004 (mpaa.org). FACT estimates that the UK entertainment industry loses over £9 billion per year through intellectual property theft, and the UK film industry £400 million (fact-uk.org). Digital film piracy has received a considerable amount of publicity in recent years. The first major case to tackle the file-sharing of films was *MGM* vs *Grokster*. Joined by twenty-eight other film companies, MGM launched a legal battle against the P2P services, Grokster and StreamCast's Morpheus, in 2003. Invoking the 1984 Supreme Court *Sony Betamax* case, the 9th US Circuit Court of Appeals ruled that file-sharing companies are not liable for users' copyright infringement. Overturned in June 2005, however, the Supreme Court decreed that those companies that actively encourage people to download free copies of music and films can be held liable for infringement. Such is the availability of film that digital piracy looks likely to remain a significant issue until relevant acts of legislation are also met with advanced encryption techniques in all of the various media forms.

Videogames

There are currently three major developments under way in the world of videogaming: the next generation of consoles; online games; and mobile gaming. Microsoft released their Xbox 360 in November 2005 and will be followed by the PlayStation 3 and Nintendo Revolution throughout 2006. On the one hand, these 256-bit consoles will see games expand in further, cinematic directions. Sony's 'Reality Synthesiser', for example, will enable advanced high-definition graphics and the PlayStation 3 will also offer a panoramic video function for use with HDTV projectors. Beneficial to the actual games and leading the further drive towards convergence, the PlayStation 3 will make use of Blu-Ray discs and will also be able to support CD-ROM, CD-RW, DVD, DVD-ROM, DVD-R and DVD+R. Although all of the consoles will offer particular advances in gaming, such as the Nintendo Revolution's introduction of wireless controllers and touch-screen functions, the PlayStation 3 is very much being sold as a total entertainment system with internet access, MP3 capabilities, video chat and digital photo imaging (see us.playstation.com; xbox.com; nintendo.com/revolution).

All of the next-generation videogame consoles are geared towards online gaming. As particularly manifest in Massively Multiplayer

Online Role-Playing Games (MMORPGs), online gaming has been said to combine the principles of gameplay with those of internet-based virtual communities. The main games in this respect have included *Counter-Strike* (2000), *Anarchy Online* (2001), *Unreal Tournament* (2002), *Ultima Online* (2003) and *Everquest* (2004) (see, for example, Ahuna 2001; Morris 2002 and 2004). The previous preserve of PCs, Microsoft's Xbox Live and the PlayStation 2's Net Play have led the way with regard to console gaming online. Offering a live, more open and thoroughly networked form of gaming, online games are much more world- rather than narrative-based. In first-person shooter form, they are based on exploration and action, and in role-playing games tend towards exploration and strategy. Where this leaves comparisons with film is difficult to ascertain, except to say that for hardcore gamers this is exactly their appeal. Online versions of console games either translate well as introductions to the complex world of online gaming, as in *Final Fantasy XI* (2004), or simply work in expanding multiplayer modes. Online games based on film series such as *Star Wars: Galaxies* (2003) and *The Matrix: Online* are particularly interesting, however, in that they combine pre-existing knowledge with more opportunity to explore the wider universe of the films.

As we have seen in Chapters 1 and 5, videogames take us through several screens. Often inspired by cinema, they can be played at home on the television or computer screen. The third development in videogaming, however, takes us beyond cinema, television and the PC. In contrast to the previous handheld gaming characterized by Nintendo's GameBoy and GameBoy Advance, current mobile gaming is also based on *connectivity*. Available on mobile phones in relatively simple retro-gaming form, the latest handheld consoles can be plugged into television sets and connected to the internet. Their primary distinction, however, is that they work through current wireless – or Wi-Fi – technology and can be played with anyone within a certain-degree radius. The mobile phone company Nokia introduced its N-Gage in 2003. Replaced by the more efficient N-Gage QD in 2004, the release of the Nintendo Dual Screen (DS) later that year and the PlayStation Portable (PSP) in 2005 have made mobile gaming a force to be reckoned with. These devices simultaneously play small-screen conversions of recent games and take players back to the basic principles of gaming (see, for example, Newman 2004: 163–9; and gamespot.com/mobile). In total, then, current developments in videogaming represent an enhancement, reconfiguration and 'reduction' of the cinematic. From the next generation of games consoles plugged into home-cinema systems to clicking away at *Metal Gear Acid* (2005) on the train, players are connected to – and through – a wider array of screens than ever before.

Micro-media

Five years after asking 'What's new about new media?', *New Media and Society* was in a position to ask 'What's changed about new media?' Co-editor Leah A. Lievrouw isolates two themes that appear to unite the responses in the collection: 'mainstreaming' and 'interiority'. Lievrouw principally relates the mainstreaming of new media to the phenomenal growth of the internet:

> One consequence of new media's mainstream status is that users' expectations about them have become at once more expansive and more routine. The continuities between conventional and new media have become more obvious, in contrast to the novelty, discontinuity, and breaks with the past that preoccupied new media scholars a decade ago. (Lievrouw 2004: 10–12)

Arguably a product of the recent familiarity with new media, 'interiority' refers to the personal made intimate. Where this can be said to have first taken place on the internet, through email, chat rooms and now instant messaging and blogs, it has also become a particular feature of current micro-media. From 'macro-scale' PCs and the internet in the 1980s and 1990s to current 'micro-scale' products such as mobile phones, iPods and Personal Digital Assistants (PDAs), micro-media is potentially much more personal and pervasive than previous new media. As Lev Manovich has addressed the rise of micro-media, where the 1990s were all about virtual space, the 2000s have indeed ended up being about our own physical spaces infiltrated by micro-gadgets and the greater flow of digital images and information:

> The previous image of a computer era – that of the VR user travelling in a virtual space – has become replaced by a new image: a person checking her e-mail or making a phone call using her personal digital assistant/ cell phone combo while at the airport, on the street, in a car, or in any other actually existing space. (Manovich 2003: 76)

The miniaturization of technology has been trumpeted since the advent of the microchip in the 1970s. What distinguishes current micro-media from micro-products of the 1970s and 1980s such as the PC and Sony Walkman, however, is that not only are current forms smaller, they are also multi-functional. The PSP, for example, is supported by the Universal Media Disc (UMD) format. Allowing the downloading of music and games from the internet, these discs also allow the possessor of the PSP to watch formatted films. Note the way in which I have referred to the 'possessor' of the PSP. Micro-media represent the final loss of distinctions relating to viewing and activity. Possessors of the PSP are certainly players but they are also users, listeners and viewers. This relates to the current marketing principle of 'anytime anywhere'. Since the introduction of the Apple iPod in 2001, for example, subsequent versions such as the iPod Shuffle and iPod Nano have become smaller and more versatile in allowing users to download and listen to music. But now there is also the iPod Video, which, as well as offering music, allows users to access music videos, short films and television episodes. Microsoft's Ultra-Mobile PC (UMPC) is also being marketed through the principle of 'Go Everywhere. Do Everything'. Developed in association with Intel and Samsung, the UMPC combines PC and PDA capabilities with film viewing and videogaming (see Green 2006; microsoft.com/windowsxp/umpc).

Looking for a way of articulating the effects of convergence on previously distinct media forms, Anna Everett has suggested the 'click' as the central activity of digital culture:

> I propose that a fetishizing of the term *click*, and its attendant iconography (the ever-present computer mouse, its onscreen arrow or white finger icon), operate through new media's lure of sensory plenitude presumably available simply, instantaneously, and pleasurably with any one of several clicking apparatuses ... As these new proliferating hardware devices saturate our physical spaces and consume our mental energies, they turn us, some argue, into either empowered posthuman cyborgs or disempowered lobotomized borgs in 'the cult of information' – that is, New Age couch potatoes. (Everett 2003: 14)

The balance here, or rather the potential schism, is ultimately that of mind and body. Existing at an intermediate sensory level, at its most effective and short-circuiting the click is the touch and the scan, the nimble finger and high-speed mind involved in accessing, organizing, interacting with and sifting through information. From PCs, TVs and DVDs to PDAs, iPods and the PSP, the click allows for speed, overload and the ability to speed through the overload. In the face of all of this, sitting down and simply watching a film in a cinema or at home can be regarded as either relatively unambitious or a chance to recharge your batteries.

Convergence

Convergence has simultaneously increased the availability of film and turned it into part of a data stream where images become information that is simply passing through. Although still concentrated in cinemas and at home, film has also become byte-sized, convenient and disposable. From watching film trailers on the internet to accessing cinema times on your mobile phone, the business of film has also become part of the flow, the previously dominant push and pull now reconfigured into something more approaching scatter and choose. As Henry Jenkins argues, convergence remains unproven. It refers to an ongoing 'process' rather than a definite 'endpoint' and, however organized the business strategies, streaming branded content across all possible outlets can also be like casting to the wind. Convergence assumes some kind of conjunction but there are now innumerable points of hit-or-miss intersection. The overall effect is that corporations have to take account of *new* consumers. From a very practical point of view, consumers are unwilling to pay for the same product more than once. Much wider than this, however, if you follow the argument that we are all in some way constructed by media, images and the business of media, then we too have become complex. As Jenkins states, this has led to a situation wherein media companies are now having to develop beyond their own previous assumptions:

> If old consumers were assumed to be passive, the new consumer is active. If old consumers were predictable and stationary, then new consumers are migratory, showing a declining loyalty to networks or even media. If old consumers were isolated individuals, then new consumers are more socially concerned. If old consumers were seen as compliant, then new consumers are resistant, taking media into their own hands. If the work of media consumers was once silent and invisible, they are now noisy and public. (Jenkins 2004: 37–8)

Starting with internal developments within film and cinema, throughout this book the case has been made for what might be termed the 'oldest' of new media. From the big screen to home viewing, cinema has always been in a state of evolution and film both low- and high-tech. The recent network of products and activities surrounding film demonstrate engagement rather than, necessarily, fragmentation. Perhaps, when everything is digital, certain distinctions won't mean as much. But, for now, film and cinema are in an important and exciting period of transition, developing, adapting and converging, leading and following, always familiar but constantly renewed.

Glossary

Analogue

The dominant material mode of operation, transmission and transcription in conventional media. In contrast to **digital** processes, analogue media work through 'mechanical' operations, 'electrical' signals and 'permanent' inscription. Using the examples of music and film, Martin Lister *et al.* refer to the 'analogous' relationship between sound waves and the grooves on a vinyl disc, and the light-sensitive image imprinted upon magnetic particles on celluloid or tape (Lister *et al.* 2003: 14). These relatively physical modes of transcription have been applied to a range of cultural and media forms: art, sculpture, the printed book, newspapers and magazines, photography, radio, film, video, and terrestrial television.

Apparatus theory

Based on the ideas of Christian Metz and Jean-Louis Baudry, and adopted by Anglo-American screen studies of the 1970s and 1980s, apparatus theory focuses on the 'physical', 'psychological' and 'political' conditions of cinema (see Baudry 1970; Metz 1974; de Lauretis and Heath 1980; Heath 1981). Combining Marxism, semiotics and psychoanalysis, apparatus theory can be regarded as an example of the 'high theory' of early Film Studies. While bringing attention round to the basic conditions of spectatorship, it did so in terms of 'captivity', 'positioning', 'restriction', 'vacancy' and 'interpellation' (see Mayne 1993; Cook and Bernink 1999: 348–9; Stam and Shohat 2000). Apparatus theory has subsequently been reconfigured to take on board the 'new apparatuses' of cinema such as home viewing, the computer screen and videogames (see, for example, Jenkins 2000; Manovich 2001; Morris 2002).

Aspect ratio

The width-to-height ratio of moving image forms. Where frame rates relate to recording and presentation (see **frames-per-second**), the aspect ratio completes that with regard to the quality, size and scope of the resulting viewing experience. The basic television and video standard is 1:33. The accepted 'Academy ratio' of cinema from 1928 to 1953 was 1:37 but the current widescreen standard in the US and UK is 1:85. CinemaScope and Cinerama can be said to have represented particular extremes with 2:35 and 2:59 respectively. These are only, however, relative aspects and where the 70mm IMAX ratio is 'only' 1:43, this doesn't take into account the absolute size or curve of respective screens (see, for example, Wollen 1993; Winston 1996; Enticknap 2005).

Bilinear filtering

A particular development of **texture mapping** within videogame graphics that allows for greater differentiation between distances. Whereas 'linear filtering' often led to the breakdown and blurring of objects approached too close or receded into the distance, bilinear filtering can distinguish between low resolution for backgrounds and higher resolution for foreground characters and objects. One of the first games to use this technique was *Quake 2* (1997) and it is now commonly used in 3D games (see Edge 2004: 91).

Bullet-time

Also known as 'flow-motion', 'flo-mo' or 'time-slicing', the bullet-time technique was popularized by *The Matrix* and works through a formation of cameras taking a cascade of shots along a 360-degree arc. The result is that of a slight freezing of time as the action is presented through a full panoramic turn. There have been many precedents to bullet-time, arguably as far back as Eadweard Muybridge's zoopraxiscope films of the late nineteenth century which involved humans and animals walking, running or galloping through a series of strings tied to individual cameras organized along a path (see Cubitt 2002 and 2004). Used in anime films such as *Akira* (1988), the technique is said to have been specifically used in live action for the first time in Michael Gondry's music video for Bjork's 'Army of Me' (1995). The technique appeared in brief moments in *Blade* (1998), *Lost in Space* (1998) and *Wing Commander* (1999), and post-*Matrix* it has variously been parodied and used in *Shrek*, *Scary Movie* (2000), *Charlie's Angels* (2000), *Swordfish* (2001) and *I, Robot* (see Kennedy 2003; Silberman 2003; Lister *et al.* 2003: 155).

Convergence

Among other uses in mathematics, computing and the social sciences, convergence is used in business to refer to consolidated organization and product ownership and licensing. It has also been applied to new media in terms of common operating systems and shared content. Conglomeration can be regarded as the most extreme convergent business practice. The AOL Time Warner merger of 2001–3 is often used as an example of the ways in which convergence cannot be 'directed' in this way, particularly when applied to new media. There is not only the question of monopoly but also the difficulty in maintaining control across so many concerns, in this case the internet, publishing, film, television and telecommunications. Rather than forcing the issue, as it were, convergence has become a 'natural' part of new media. This applies to matters of both form and content: of multimedia PCs and videogame consoles, for example; increasingly common digital aesthetics; and branded content made available across numerous media platforms (see Boddy 2003; Gitlin 2003; Murray 2003; Jenkins 2004; Miller 2004).

Cyberculture studies

The study of control and communication in computer-based media and culture. Cyberculture Studies first began by looking at the commercial advances and subcultural uses of computer-based technology in the 1980s, its use of the term 'cyber' derived from the scientific field of cybernetics and applied to numerous concepts as 'cyborgs', 'cyberspace' and 'cyberpunk'. Following the growth of computer-based technologies in the 1990s, Cyberculture Studies became an identifiable academic field of study and progressed to 'virtual' concepts such as 'virtual reality' and 'virtual communities'. Almost science fiction in some of its speculations, Cyberculture Studies has nevertheless provided key foundations for looking at current developments in digital media (see, for example, Dery 1994 and 1996; Bell and Kennedy 2000; and Bell 2001).

Digital

The dominant mode of operation and representation in new media forms and technologies. Where **analogue** media are said to work through 'material' processes, digital media work through 'mathematical' processes as aggregates of binary numbers result in images, signals and sound. As Martin Lister *et al.* state, the principles of 'addition, subtraction, multiplication and division' (Lister *et al.* 2003: 15) are very much key to digital media's advantages over analogue in terms of 'infinite' manipulation and conversion. The digital has been applied to: traditional media such as photography, radio, film, cinema and television; new media as in computers, the internet, videogames and micro-media; and, in more widespread terms, 'digital culture' and 'the digital revolution'.

Frames-per-second (fps)

The speed at which devices capture, project and transmit images. Often used in association with the **aspect ratio**, these are said to determine the perceived quality of moving images; 35mm film is regarded as the professional standard at 24 fps. Traditional 'interlaced' video, which alternates between the 'odd' and 'even' scanning of images, works at 60 fps and modern 'progressive' video, which combines the two fields within each frame, up to 25 fps (see, for example, Winston 1996; Enticknap 2005). Part of the versatility of digital video is that it is able to alternate between 60 and 25 fps. Conventional television works at 60 fps but recent digital and HD television work at 25. Computer screens and videogames are more correctly determined in terms of 'output' and 'refresh' rates rather than input, and can offer between 60 and 25 fps.

High-definition (HD)

An advanced system that allows for the greater compression, storage and resolution of data and images than analogue media and current digital video, digital television and DVDs. High-definition television was first developed in Japan in the 1980s and promoted through the international Telecommunications Act of 1996. HDTV offers two to four times the image resolution of the standard television systems, NTSC, SECAM and PAL. High-definition cameras and the HDTV process have come to be used in recent filmmaking, and high-definition Blu-Ray and HD-DV discs are being introduced as a potential successor to DVDs.

Ludology

The study of the essential properties of play. Articulated through the so-called **narratology** versus ludology debate within Game Studies, where narrative is said to provide for author-centred rules and structures, play is much more open and democratic. Although games may well proceed according to certain rules, players have to work in actively developing appropriate skills and strategies that will result in them winning out over the game or other players (see Aarseth 2001; Juul 2001; Frasca 2003a and 2003b).

Motion capture

A technique that works in capturing an actor's physical performance as a 'reference point' for digitally rendered characters in films and videogames. The actor wears a mono-coloured suit equipped with motion sensors which allow the computer to track and store movement. This is often supplemented by 'facial capture' to give the character expressive capabilities (see Creed 2000; Wolf 2003b; North 2005). The combination of motion capture and facial capture has come to be known as 'performance capture'. This was first used in relation to the animated feature film, *The Polar Express* (2004).

Motion control

In its analogue form, motion control refers to a technique pioneered by *Star Wars* whereby a computer-controlled camera tracks one special effects element (e.g. a spaceship) and is able to repeat exactly the same moves in relation to other elements (e.g. backdrops and more spaceships). These multiple elements are then combined to create dynamic special effects shots. This is also paramount in digital special effects sequences where the camera remains dynamic and consistent across a greater range of live and virtual elements. This also reaches the point where the camera itself is virtual (see **virtual cinematography**).

Narratology

The study of narrative and narrative structure in literary, film and media texts. Derived from literary studies, narratology looks at numerous elements such as: archetypes, genre, plot and story, dramatic structure, narrative techniques, point of view, characters and characterization. David Bordwell's influential *Narration in the Fiction Film* (1985) distinguishes between 'narrative' and 'narration' in terms of 'process' and 'activity', principally the ways in which film viewers are also involved in the construction of narrative meaning (Bordwell 1985: 29–47). Bordwell's study is also important in that it looks at the spatial, rather than solely temporal properties of film narrative (Bordwell 1985: 48–62). New Media Studies has often distinguished itself in terms of narrative in that computer culture works through primarily spatial operations and levels of interactivity (see, for example, Manovich 2001). See **ludology**.

Texture mapping

A major development in videogame graphics that has allowed for smoother and more varied textures in 3D games. As particularly applied to locations and environments rendered in real-time, the effect is of a greater solidity to settings and more convincing use of perspective. The first major step away from 'point-sampled' pixels that led to a breakdown in images close up or at a distance, three of the first games to use texture mapping were *Wolfenstein 3D* (1992), *Ultima Underworld* (1992) and *Magic Carpet* (1994) (see Edge 2004: 87).

Vector graphics

Referred to as geometric modelling within computer design, vector graphics were a popular form of representation in videogames of the late 1970s and early 1980s. Replacing 'raster' dots with 'wireframe' lines, vector graphics allowed smoother navigation through empty spaces. The technique was first used in scrolling 2D form in *Lunar Lander* (1979) and *Asteroids* (1979), and then in first-person 3D games such as *Battlezone* (1980) and *Star Wars* (1983). The first 3D wireframe game to feature polygon-filled graphics was *I, Robot* (1983) (see Poole 2000; McMahan 2003; Wolf 2003a).

Virtual cinematography

Also known as 'virtual cinema', 'universal capture' or 'u-cap', virtual cinematography works through the complete simulation of filmmaking techniques such as cinematography and editing, and live-action elements such as actors and sets. The result is that of entire sequences that seamlessly combine live and virtual elements, to the accelerated extent where the virtual camera, virtual actors and virtual sets fully take over in certain parts of the entire sequence. The technique was first developed by George Borshukov who used image-based modelling and rendering to create a photorealistic aerial flight over the UC Berkeley campus in his *Campanile Movie* (1997). After working together on the **bullet-time** sequences in *The Matrix*, Borshukov and senior visual effects supervisor John Gaeta made extensive use of virtual cinematography in *The Matrix Reloaded* and *The Matrix Revolutions* (see Silberman 2003; North 2005).

Virtual sets

Film sets that are either supplemented or completely composed of green-screen backdrops which allow for computer-generated locations and environments to be added in postproduction. This is used extensively in science fiction and fantasy blockbusters, and live-action films entirely composed of virtual sets have included *Immortel (ad vitam)* (2004), *Sky Captain the World of Tomorrow* (2004), *Casshern* (2004) and *Sin City*. 'Virtual studios' are pre-production versions of virtual sets and allow directors to walk through virtual versions of the sets in order to plan shots and scenes.

Notes

Chapter 2

1. Quoted from the television documentary, *Power to the Pixel* (UK, Channel 4, 9/10/01).
2. See Figgis's Video Diary and Audio Commentary on the *Timecode* DVD. The DVD also includes the first test version of the film and an Interactive Audio Mix that allows viewers to isolate the sound on each of the four screens.
3. Taken from the DVD Commentary by Evans and Finn. The DVD also offers an Interactive Mode that presents the film as if displayed on a computer screen and is most effective when played on a laptop. Adopting a webpage format, the main window follows the film and the five 'player' icons are presented down the right-hand side of the screen, their odds of survival continually fluctuating. The viewer-user can also access Archive Footage, the full Audition Tapes and two further special features are the Multi Camera option, which enables the choice of camera angles on four selected scenes, and a chilling Audio Commentary by 'The Company'.
4. See the DVD documentary, *Pure Rage: The Making of 28 Days Later*. See also the Audio Commentary by Boyle and writer Alex Garland.

Chapter 3

1. See, for example, the web documentary, '"Reel 6": Creating the Action in the Geonosis Arena', on the *Attack of the Clones* DVD. Reel 6 is highlighted in the commentaries to all of the original and prequel DVDs but expressly so in relation to Episode II where it is regarded as particularly intensive in terms of action, construction, sound and effects.
2. Quoted from the Special Extended DVD documentary, *The Taming of Smeagol*. As well as the documentary itself, technical information on the development and realization of Gollum can be found in the 'Andy Serkis Animation Reference', 'Gollum's "Stand In"' and 'Design Gallery' features.

Chapter 4

1. Other notable *Star Wars* fan sites include supershadow.com, starwarschicks.com and starwarz.com.
2. See also, comics2film.com, superherotimes.com and comicbookresources.com.
3. See, for example, 'Frank Miller (an unofficial homepage)' at hem.passagen.se/fm4; 'The Complete Works of Frank Miller' at moebiusgraphics.com; and the recent frankmillerfanclub.tribe.net.
4. This is based on looking at the first fifty member profiles on the 'Sin City? Sexist City' (16/4/05) thread. Not all members state their years of birth but of the twenty-seven that do, all are born between 1982 and 1989, the average being 1984. Older members may well not choose to highlight their ages but we can assume a slightly higher average for this adult-oriented film. For a more reliable figure relating to *Star Wars* fans, see the 'How old are you?' (15/7/03) poll on TFN. Of the 5000 votes, 24 per cent were 12–17 years old, 33 per cent 18–24 and 34 per cent 25–34.

Chapter 5

1. The most useful online sources for the study of videogames and game culture are: gamestudies.org; game-culture.com; joystick101.org; ludology.org; and digiplay.org.uk.
2. Gamespot.com is the most extensive site relating to videogame news and reviews. For consideration of how players regard film tie-ins, Gamespot allows for Player Reviews of individual titles and provides a list of the Most Popular games based on search traffic. On the whole, Player Reviews score higher for film-related games and tend to favour presentation over advanced gameplay. The Most Popular list also demonstrates greater interest in these games. In contrast to the three film tie-ins featured in the Top Rated list, for example, the Most Popular featured ten for the same period.
3. See the documentary, *The Hollywood Game: The Making of Metal Gear Solid 2*, featured on the bonus DVD included with the European release of the game. Kojima's cinematic influences are also mentioned in the CODEC conversations between Raiden (real name Jack) and Rose throughout the game. The Metal Gear Ray was influenced by King Kong- and Godzilla-style monster movies, and, given the game's predominant ocean locations, Jack and Rose are a nod to James Cameron's *Titanic*.

Chapter 6

1. Quoted from the *Reloaded* DVD feature, *The Matrix Unfolds*.
2. There are numerous online sources relating to the philosophical aspects of the *Matrix* films. See, in particular, the Philosophy section of the Mainframe at whatisthematrix.com. The most valuable fan sites in this respect include matrixfans.net and thematrix101.com.
3. The short documentary *What is Bullet Time?* was included with the VHS and DVD releases of *The Matrix*. See, also, the Bullet Time Walk Through and interview with visual effects supervisor, John Gaeta, on the *Matrix* VFX section at whatisthematrix.com.
4. Quoted from the *Reloaded* DVD documentary, *Preload*.
5. See, in particular, technical designer George Borshukov's extensive website, virtualcinematography.org. The technique is also covered in relation to the main set-pieces of the sequels. See the *Reloaded* VFX section of whatisthematrix.com; the *Reloaded* DVD feature, *The Freeway Chase*; and the *Revolutions* DVD feature, *CG Revolution*.
6. Quoted from the *Reloaded* DVD feature, *Get Me An Exit*.
7. See, in particular, the *Animatrix* DVD documentary, *Scrolls to Screen: The History and Culture of Anime*.
8. Taking the average of Gamespot's Player and Critic reviews, gamespot.com rates the *Matrix* games as follows: *The Matrix: Path of Neo* 7.4 ('good'); *The Matrix: Online* 7.2 ('good'); and *Enter the Matrix* 6.7 ('fair').

Bibliography

Aarseth, E.J. (2001) 'Computer Game Studies, Year One', *Game Studies* Issue 1 (July), available online at: <http://www.gamestudies.org/0101/editorial.html>

Acland, C.R. (2003) *Screen Traffic: Movies, Multiplexes, and Global Culture*. London and Durham, NC: Duke University Press

Ahuna, C. (2001) 'Online Game Communities are Social in Nature', available online at: <http://switch.sjsu.edu/v7n1/articles/cindy02.html>

Aloi, P. (2005) 'Beyond the Blair Witch: A New Horror Aesthetic?' in G. King, ed., *The Spectacle of the Real: From Hollywood to Reality TV and Beyond*, pp. 187–200. Bristol and Portland: Intellect

Allen, M. (1998) 'From *Bwana Devil* to *Batman Forever*: Technology in Contemporary Hollywood Cinema' in S. Neale and M. Smith, eds, *Contemporary Hollywood Cinema*, pp. 109–29. London and New York: Routledge

Allen, M. (2002) 'The Impact of Digital Technologies on Film Aesthetics' in D. Harries, ed., *The New Media Book*, pp. 109–18. London: BFI

Allen, M. (2003) *Contemporary US Cinema*. London: Pearson

Askwith, I. (2003) 'A Matrix in Every Medium', available online at: <http://www.salon.com/tech/feature/2003/05/12/matrix-universe>

Bacon-Smith, C. (1992) *Enterprising Women: Television Fandom and the Creation of Popular Myth*. Philadelphia: University of Pennsylvania Press

Baker, R. (1993) 'Computer Technology and Special Effects in Contemporary Cinema' in P. Hayward and T. Wollen, eds, *Future Visions: New Technologies of the Screen*, pp. 31–45. London: BFI

Balides, C. (2003) 'Immersion in the Virtual Ornament: Contemporary "Movie Ride" Films' in D. Thorburn and H. Jenkins, eds, *Rethinking Media Change: The Aesthetics of Transition*, pp. 315–36. Cambridge, MA, and London: MIT

Balio, T. (1985), ed., *The American Film Industry*. Madison: University of Wisconsin Press

Balio, T. (1990), ed., *Hollywood in the Age of Television*. Boston, MA: Unwin Hyman

Barker, M. (2000) *From Antz to Titanic: Reinventing Film Analysis*. London: Pluto

Barker, M. (2004) 'News, Reviews, Interviews and Other Ancillary Materials – A Critique and Research Proposal', *Scope: An Online Journal of Film Studies* (February), available online at: <http:///www.nottingham.ac.uk/film/journal/articles/news-reviews.htm>

Baudry, J.-L. (1970) 'Ideological Effects of the Basic Cinematographic Apparatus' in G. Mast *et al.*, eds, *Film Theory and Criticism: Introductory Readings* 4th edn. Oxford: Oxford University Press, 1992

Bazin, A. (1967) *What is Cinema?* Berkeley and Los Angeles: University of California Press

Beck, J.C. (2004) 'The Concept of Narrative: An Analysis of *Requiem for a Dream* (.com) and *Donnie Darko* (.com)', *Convergence* Vol. 10, No. 3 (autumn), pp. 55–82

Bell, D. (2001) *An Introduction to Cybercultures*. London and New York: Routledge

Bell, D. and Kennedy, B. (2000) *The Cybercultures Reader*. London and New York: Routledge

Belton, J. (1988) 'CinemaScope and Historical Methodology' reprt in T. Schatz, ed., *Hollywood: Critical Concepts in Media and Cultural Studies, Volume III (Social Dimensions: Technology, Regulation and Audience)*, pp. 27–50. London and New York: Routledge, 2004

Belton, J. (1992) *Widescreen Cinema*. Cambridge, MA: Harvard University Press

Binkley, T. (1993) 'Refiguring Culture' in P. Hayward and T. Wollen, eds, *Future Visions: New Technologies of the Screen*, pp. 92–122. London: BFI

Boddy, W. (2000) 'Weather Porn and the Battle for Eyeballs: Promoting Digital Television in the USA and UK' in J. Fullerton and A.S. Widding, eds, *Moving Images: From Edison to the Webcam*, pp. 133–47. London, Paris, Rome, Sydney: John Libbey

Boddy, W. (2002) 'New Media as Old Media: Television' in D. Harries, ed., *The New Media Book*, pp. 242–53. London: BFI

Boddy, W. (2003) 'Redefining the Home Screen: Technological Convergence as Trauma and Business Plan' in D. Thorburn and H. Jenkins, eds, *Rethinking Media Change: The Aesthetics of Transition*, pp. 191–200. Cambridge, MA, and London: MIT

Bolter, J.D. and Grusin, R. (1999) *Remediation: Understanding New Media*. Cambridge, MA, and London: MIT

Bordwell, D. (1985) *Narration in the Fiction Film*. London: Methuen

Brodesser, C. and Fritz, B. (2005) 'Halo, Hollywood', *Variety*, 3 Feb., available online at: <http://www.variety.com/article/VR1117917399?categoryid=1079&cs=1>

Brooker, W. (1997) 'New Hope: The Postmodern Project of *Star Wars*' in P. Brooker and W. Brooker, eds, *Postmodern After-Images: A Reader in Film, Television and Video*, pp. 101–12. London: Arnold

Brooker, W. (2002) *Using the Force: Creativity, Community and Star Wars Fans*. New York and London: Continuum

Brooker, W. (2003) 'Conclusion: Overflow and Audience' in W. Brooker and D. Jermyn, eds, *The Audience Studies Reader*, pp. 322–34. London and New York: Routledge

Brooker, W. and Jermyn, D. (2003), eds, *The Audience Studies Reader*. London and New York: Routledge

Buckland, W. (1999) 'Between Science Fact and Science Fiction: Spielberg's Digital Dinosaurs, Possible Worlds, and the New Aesthetic Realism', *Screen* Vol. 40, No. 2 (summer), pp. 177–92

Buckland, W. (2000) 'Video Pleasure and Narrative Cinema: Luc Besson's *The Fifth Element* and Video Game Logic' in J. Fullerton and A.S. Widding, eds, *Moving Images: From Edison to the Webcam*, pp. 159–64. London, Paris and Rome: John Libbey

Bukatman, S. (1993) *Terminal Identity: The Virtual Subject in Postmodern Science Fiction*. Durham, NC and London: Duke University Press

Bukatman, S. (2003) *Matters of Gravity: Special Effects and Supermen in the 20th Century*. Durham, NC and London: Duke University Press

Burnett, R. and Marshall, P.D. (2003) *Web Theory: An Introduction*. London and New York: Routledge

Butler, J.G. (2002) 'The Internet and the World Wide Web' in D. Harries, ed., *The New Media Book*, pp. 40–51. London: BFI

Caldwell, J.T. (1995) *Televisuality: Style, Crisis, and Authority in American Television*. New Brunswick, NJ: Rutgers University Press

Caldwell, J. T. (2003) 'Second-Shift Media Aesthetics: Programming, Interactivity, and User Flows' in A. Everett and J. T. Caldwell, eds, *New Media: Theories and Practices of Digitextuality*, pp. 127–44. New York and London: Routledge

Carr, D. (2003) 'Play Dead: Genre and Affect in *Silent Hill* and *Planescape Torment*', *Game Studies* Vol. 3, Issue 1 (May), available online at: <http://www.gamestudies.org/ 0301/carr/>

Carr, D. (2005) 'The Rules of the Game, The Burden of Narrative: *Enter the Matrix*' in S. Gillis, ed., *The Matrix Trilogy: Cyberpunk Reloaded*, pp. 36–47. London and New York: Wallflower

Caughie, J. and Cubitt, S. (1999), eds, 'CGI, FX and the Question of Cinema', *Screen* Special Issue, Vol. 40, No. 2 (summer)

Cavallaro, D. (2000) *Cyberpunk and Cyberculture*. London: Athlone

Chaudhuri, S. (2005) 'Dogma Brothers: Lars Von Trier and Thomas Vinterberg' in N. Rombes, ed., *New Punk Cinema*, pp.153–67. Edinburgh: Edinburgh University Press

Chesher, C. (2004) 'Neither Gaze nor Glance, but Glaze: Relating to Console Game Screens', *Journal of media arts culture*, Vol. 1, No. 1

(January), available online at: <http://www.scan.net.au/scan/journal/display_article.php?recordID=19>

Chin, B. and Gray, J. (2001) ''One Ring to Rule Them All': Pre-viewers and Pre-Texts of the *Lord of the Rings* films', *Intensities: The Journal of Cult Media* Issue 2 (autumn/winter), available online at: <<http://www.cult-media.com/issue2/Achingray.htm>>

Clerc, S. (1996) 'Estrogen Brigades and 'Big Tits' Threads: Media Fandom On-Line and Off', in L. Cherny and E. Reba Weise, eds, *Wired_Women: Gender and New Realities in Cyberspace*. Seattle: Seal Press

Cook, D.A. (2004) *A History of Narrative Film*, 4th edn. New York: Norton

Cook, P. and Bernink, M. (1999), eds, *The Cinema Book* 2nd edn. London: BFI

Crawford, C. (2003) 'Interactive Storytelling' in M.J.P. Wolf and B. Perron, eds, *The Video Game Theory Reader*, pp. 259–73. New York and London: Routledge

Creed, B. (2000) 'The Cyberstar: Digital Pleasures and the End of the Unconscious', *Screen*, Vol. 41, No. 1 (spring), pp. 79–86

Crogan, P. (2003) 'Gametime: History, Narrative, and Temporality in *Combat Flight Simulator*' in M.J.P. Wolf and B. Perron, eds, *The Video Game Theory Reader*, pp. 275–301. New York and London: Routledge

Cubitt, S. (2002) 'Digital Filming and Special Effects' in D. Harries, ed., *The New Media Book*, pp. 17–29. London: BFI

Cubitt, S. (2004) *The Cinema Effect*. Cambridge, MA, and London: MIT

Culkin, N. and Randle, K. (2003) 'Digital Cinema: Opportunities and Challenges', *Convergence* Vol. 9, No. 4 (winter), pp. 79–98

Darley, A. (2000) *Visual Digital Culture: Surface Play in New Media Genres*. London and New York: Routledge

de Lauretis, T. and Heath, S. (1980), eds, *The Cinematic Apparatus*. London and Basingstoke: Macmillan

Dery, M. (1994), ed., *Flame Wars: The Discourse of Cyberculture*. Durham, NC and London: Duke University Press

Dery, M. (1996) *Escape Velocity: Cyberculture at the End of the Century*. London: Hodder and Stoughton

Dixon, W.W. (2003) *Visions of the Apocalypse: Spectacles of Destruction in American Cinema*. London and New York: Wallflower

Dobie, I. (2004) 'The Music Industry versus the Internet: MP3 and Other Cyber Music Wars' in D. Gauntlett and R. Harley, eds, *Web.Studies* 2nd edn., pp. 204–13. London: Arnold

Edge (2000) 'The 100 Best Games of All Time', Issue 80 (January), pp. 53–71

Edge (2004) 'The New Black', Issue 136 (May), pp. 84–91

Ellis, J. (1982) *Visible Fictions: Cinema, Television, Video*. London: Routledge

ELSPA (2004) 'Video Games Market Demonstrates Over 100 Per Cent Growth in Six Years', 1 Sept., available online at: <http://www.elspa.com/about /pr/pr.asp? mode= view&t=1&id=478>

ELSPA (2005) 'UK Software Market Tops the Charts Yet Again', 10 Jan., available online at: <http://www.elspa.com/about/pr/pr.asp?mode= view&t=1&id=516>

Enticknap, L. (2005) *Moving Image Technology: From Zoetrope to Digital.* London and New York: Wallflower

Everett, A. (2003) 'Digitextuality and Click Theory: Theses on Convergence Media in the Digital Age' in A. Everett and J.T. Caldwell, eds, *New Media: Theories and Practices of Digitextuality*, pp. 3–28. New York and London: Routledge

Everett, A. and Caldwell, J.T. (2003), eds, *New Media: Theories and Practices of Digitextuality.* New York and London: Routledge

Fiske, John (1987) *Television Culture.* London: Routledge

Fiske, J. (1992) 'The Cultural Economy of Fandom' in L.A. Lewis, ed., *The Adoring Audience: Fan Culture and Popular Media.* London and New York: Routledge

Frasca, G. (2003a) 'Simulation versus Narrative: Introduction to Ludology' in M.J.P. Wolf and B. Perron, eds, *The Video Game Theory Reader*, pp. 221–35. New York and London: Routledge

Frasca, G. (2003b) 'Ludologists Love Stories, too: Notes from a Debate that Never Took Place', available online at: <http://ludology.org/articles/Frasca_LevelUp2003>

Friedberg, A. (2000) 'The End of Cinema: Multi-media and Technological Change' in C. Gledhill and L. Williams, eds, *Reinventing Film Studies*, pp. 438–53. London: Arnold

Friedberg, A. (2002) 'CD and DVD' in D. Harries, ed., *The New Media Book*, pp. 30–9. London: BFI

Friedman, T. (1995) 'Making Sense of Software: Computer Games and Interactive Textuality' in S.G. Jones, ed., *Cybersociety: Computer-Mediated Communication and Community*, pp. 73–89. London: Sage

Fritz, B. (2005) 'B.O. Plays Slip 'n' Slide', *Variety 29* Dec., available online at: <http://www.variety.com/article/VR1117935318?categoryid=10&cs=1>

Fritz, B. and McNary, D. (2004) 'H'Wood Gets Back in Game', *Variety* 24 Oct., available online at: <http://www.variety.com/article/VR1117912364?categoryid=1079& cs=1>

Fuller, M. and Jenkins, H. (1995) 'Nintendo and New World Travel Writing: A Dialogue' in S.G. Jones, ed., *Cybersociety: Computer-Mediated Communication and Community*, pp. 57–72. London: Sage

games™ (2004) Review of *Metal Gear Solid 3: Snake Eater*, Issue 27, pp. 92–5

Gerstmann, J. (2003) Review of *Enter the Matrix*, available online at: <http://www.gamespot.com/ps2/action/enterthematrix/review-2.html>

Gitlin, T. (2003) *Media Unlimited*. New York: Owl Books

Gomery, D. (1980) 'Towards an Economic History of the Cinema: The Coming of Sound in Hollywood' in T. de Lauretis and S. Heath, eds, *The Cinematic Apparatus*, pp. 38–46. London and Basingstoke: Macmillan

Gomery, D. (2003) 'The Hollywood Blockbuster: Industrial Analysis and Practice' in J. Stringer, ed., *Hollywood Blockbusters*, pp. 72–83. London and New York: Routledge

Gray, J. (2003) 'New Audiences, New Textualities: Anti-Fans and Non-Fans', *International Journal of Cultural Studies*, Vol. 6, No. 1, pp. 64–81

Green, C. (2006) 'All Systems Go to Join the Convergence Game', *Screen International* No.1540 (March 17–23), pp. 4–7

Grieb, M. (2002) 'Run Lara Run' in G. King and T. Krzywinska, eds, *Screenplay: Cinema/Videogames/Interfaces*, pp. 157–70. London and New York: Wallflower

Griffiths, K. (2003) 'The Manipulated Image', *Convergence* Vol. 9, No. 4 (winter), pp.12–26

Gurak, L.J. (2004) 'Internet Studies in the Twenty-First Century' in D. Gauntlett and R. Harley, eds, *Web.Studies* 2nd edn., pp. 24–33. London: Arnold

Haber, K. (2003), ed., *Exploring The Matrix: New Writings on The Matrix and the Cyber Future*. London: ibooks

Haley, G. (2001) 'A.I. Advertising Intelligence', *SFX* Issue 82 (September), p. 41

Hanson, M. (2003) *The End of Celluloid: Film Futures in the Digital Age*. Mies and Hove: RotoVision

Harbord, Janet (2002) *Film Cultures*. London, Thousand Oaks, New Delhi: Sage

Harley, R. (1999), ed., Special Issue, 'Before and after Cinema', *Convergence* Vol. 5, No. 2 (summer)

Harper, G. (2005) 'DVD and the New Cinema of Complexity' in N. Rombes, ed., *New Punk Cinema*. Edinburgh: Edinburgh University Press

Harris, C. and Alexander, A. (1998), eds, *Theorizing Fandom: Fans, Subculture and Identity*. Cresskill, NJ: Hampton Press

Harries, D. ed., (2002a), *The New Media Book*. London: BFI

Harries, D. (2002b) 'Watching the Internet' in D. Harries, ed., *The New Media Book*, pp. 171–82. London: BFI

Hazleton, J. (2006) 'Rivals Line up for Battle', *Screen International* No.1540 (March 17–23), pp. 14–15

Heath, S. (1976) 'On Screen, in Frame: Film and Ideology' in S. Heath, *Questions of Cinema*, pp. 1–18. Bloomington: Indiana University Press, 1981

Heath, S. (1980) 'The Cinematic Apparatus: Technology as Historical and Cultural Form' in T. de Lauretis and S. Heath, eds, *The Cinematic Apparatus*, pp. 1–13. London and Basingstoke: Macmillan

Heath, S. (1981) *Questions of Cinema*. Bloomington: Indiana University Press

Herrold, A. (2003) 'The Future of Digital Cinema in Europe: A Legal Challenge for the EU?', *Convergence* Vol. 9, No. 4 (winter), pp. 99–110

Herz, J.C. (1997) *Joystick Nation: How Video Games Ate Our Quarters, Won Our Hearts, and Rewired Our Minds*. Boston, MA: Little, Brown

Hewitt, C. (2003) 'Is Rental Dead?', *Empire* Issue 166 (April), pp. 136–7

Higgins, S. (2003) 'A New Colour Consciousness: Colour in the Digital Age', *Convergence* Vol. 9, No. 4 (winter), pp. 60–76

Hills, M. (2001) 'Virtually out There: Strategies, Tactics and Affective Spaces in On-Line Fandom' in S.R. Munt, ed., *Technospaces: Inside the New Media*, pp. 147–60. London and New York: Continuum

Hills, M. (2002) *Fan Cultures*. London and New York: Routledge

Hilmes, M. (2002) 'Cable, Satellite and Digital Technologies' in D. Harries, ed., *The New Media Book*, pp. 4–16. London: BFI

Howells, S.A. (2002) 'Watching a Game, Playing a Movie: When Media Collide' in G. King and T. Krzywinska, eds, *Screenplay: Cinema/Videogames/Interfaces*, pp. 110–21. London and New York: Wallflower

Hughes, D. (2003) *Comic Book Movies*. London: Virgin

Hunt, L. (2002) ''I Know Kung Fu!' The Martial Arts in the Age of Digital Reproduction' in G. King and T. Krzywinska, eds, *Screenplay: Cinema/Videogames/Interfaces*, pp. 194–205. London and New York: Wallflower

Hunter, Sandy (2003), '28 Days Later: An Interview with Danny Boyle', available online at: <http://www.res.com/magazine/articles/28dayslateraninterviewwithdannyboyle_2003-05-21.html>

Irwin, W. (2002), ed., *The Matrix and Philosophy: Welcome to the Desert of the Real*. LaSalle: Open Court

Jancovich, M., Faire, L. and Stubbings, S. (2003) *The Place of the Audience: Cultural Geographies of Film Consumption*. London: BFI

Jenkins, H. (1992) *Textual Poachers: Television Fans and Participatory Culture*. London and New York: Routledge

Jenkins, H. (2000) 'Reception Theory and Audience Research: The Mystery of the Vampire's Kiss' in C. Geldhill and L. Williams, eds, *Reinventing Film Studies*, pp. 165–82. London: Arnold

Jenkins, H. (2001) 'Thoughts on Tomb Raider and Final Fantasy' available online at: <http://www.joystick101.org/?op=displaystory&sid=2001/7/27/135553/338>

Jenkins, H. (2002) 'Interactive Audiences?' in D. Harries, ed., *The New Media Book*, pp. 157–70. London: BFI

Jenkins, H. (2003) '*Quentin Tarantino's Star Wars?* Digital Cinema, Media Convergence, and Participatory Culture' in D. Thorburn and H. Jenkins, eds, *Rethinking Media Change: The Aesthetics of Transition*, pp. 281–312. Cambridge, MA, and London: MIT

Jenkins, H. (2004) 'The Cultural Logic of Convergence', *International Journal of Cultural Studies*, Vol. 7, No. 1, pp. 33–43

Jones, S.G. (2002) 'Phantom Menace: Killer Fans, Consumer Activism and Digital Filmmakers' in X. Mendik and S.J. Schneider, eds, *Underground USA: Filmmaking Beyond the Hollywood Canon*. London and New York: Wallflower

Jordan, T. (1999) *Cyberpower: The Culture and Politics of the Internet*. London and New York: Routledge

Juul, J. (2001) 'Games Telling Stories? – A Brief Note on Games and Narratives', *Game Studies* Issue 1 (July), available online at: <http://www.gamestudies.org/0101/juul-gts/>

Kasavian, G. (2001) Review of *Metal Gear Solid 2: Sons of Liberty*, available online at: <http://www.gamespot.com/ps2/adventure/metalgearsolid2sonsol/review.html>

Keane, S. (2000) 'Event Horizons: Nostalgic Experience in *Star Wars* and the Special Edition' in J. Hallam and N. Moody, eds, *Consuming for Pleasure: Selected Essays on Popular Fictions*, pp. 314–33. Liverpool: John Moores University Press

Keane, S. (2002) 'From Hardware to Fleshware: Plugging into David Cronenberg's *eXistenZ*', in G. King and T. Krzywinska, eds, *Screenplay: Cinema/Videogames/ Interfaces*, pp. 145–56. London and New York: Wallflower

Keane, S. (2006) *Disaster Movies: The Cinema of Catastrophe*, 2nd edn. London and New York: Wallflower

Kennedy, C. (2003) 'Seeing is Believing', *Empire* Issue 168 (June), pp. 80–95

Kent, S.L. (2001) 'Super Mario Nation' in M.J.P. Wolf, ed., *The Medium of the Video Game*, pp. 35–48. Austin: University of Texas Press

Kilday, G. (2006) 'MPAA's '05 scorecard: B.O. slips, costs stabilize', *Hollywood Reporter* 10 Mar., available online at: <http://www.hollywoodreporter.com/thr/film/article_display.jsp?vnu_content_id=1002156202>

Kinder, M. (1991) *Playing with Power in Movies, Television, and Video Games: From Muppet Babies to Teenage Mutant Ninja Turtles*. Berkeley, Los Angeles, and London: University of California Press

Kinder, M. (2002) 'Narrative Equivocations between Movies and Games' in D. Harries, ed., *The New Media Book*, pp. 119–32. London: BFI

King, G. (2000) *Spectacular Narratives: Hollywood in the Age of the Blockbuster*. London and New York: I.B. Tauris

King, G. (2002) *New Hollywood Cinema: An Introduction*. London and New York: I.B. Tauris

King, G. (2005) *American Independent Cinema*. London and New York: I.B. Tauris

King, G. and Krzywinska, T. (2000) *Science Fiction Cinema: From Outerspace to Cyberspace*. London: Wallflower

King, G. and Krzywinska, T. (2002), eds, *Screenplay: Cinema/Videogames/ Interfaces*. London and New York: Wallflower

Klinger, B. (1998) 'The New Media Aristocrats: Home Theater and the Domestic Film Experience' reprd in T. Schatz, ed., *Hollywood: Critical Concepts in Media and Cultural Studies Volume III*, pp. 391–411. London and New York: Routledge, 2004

Klinger, B. (2001) 'The Contemporary Cinephile: Film Collecting in the Post-Video Era' in M. Stokes and R. Maltby, eds, *Hollywood Spectatorship: Changing Perceptions of Cinema Audiences*, pp. 132–51. London: BFI

Knowles, H. (2002) *Ain't It Cool?: Kicking Hollywood's Butt*. London: Boxtree

Kramer, P. (2003) '"Want to Take a Ride?" Reflections on the Blockbuster Experience in *Contact* (1997)' in J. Stringer, ed., *Movie Blockbusters*, pp. 128–40. London and New York: Routledge

Krzywinska, T. (2002) 'Hands-On Horror' in G. King and T. Krzywinska, eds, *Screenplay: Cinema/Videogames/Interfaces*, pp. 206–23. London and New York: Wallflower

Lancaster, K. (2001) *Interacting with Babylon 5: Fan Performances in a Media Universe*. Austin: University of Texas Press

Lancaster, K. and Mikotowicz, T. (2001), eds, *Performing the Force: Essays on Immersion into Science Fiction, Fantasy and Horror Environments*. Jefferson: McFarland

Landon, B. (1992) *The Aesthetics of Ambivalence: Rethinking Science Fiction Film in the Age of Electronic (Re)Production*. Westport, Connecticut, and London: Greenwood

Laurel, B. (1993) *Computers as Theater*. London: Addison-Wesley

Lawrence, M. (2004) *Like a Splinter in Your Mind: The Philosophy behind the Matrix Trilogy*. Oxford: Blackwell

Lewis, J. (1998), ed., *The New American Cinema*. Durham, NC and London: Duke University Press

Lewis, J. (2003) 'Following the Money in America's Sunniest Town: Some Notes on the Political Economy of the Hollywood Blockbuster' in J. Stringer, ed., *Hollywood Blockbusters*, pp. 61–71. London and New York: Routledge

Lewis, L.A. (1992), ed., *The Adoring Audience: Fan Culture and Popular Media*. London and New York: Routledge

Lievrouw, L.A. (2004) 'What's Changed about New Media? Introduction to the Fifth Anniversary Issue of *new media and society*', *New Media and Society* Vol. 6, No. 1 (February), pp. 9–15

Lister, M. (1995), ed., *The Photographic Image in Digital Culture*. London and New York: Routledge

Lister, M., Dovey, J., Giddings, S., Grant, I. and Kelly, K. (2003), eds, *New Media: A Critical Introduction*. London and New York: Routledge

Lunenfeld, P. (1999), ed., *The Digital Dialectic: New Essays on New Media*. Cambridge, MA, and London: MIT

McCarthy, T. (1999) Review of *The Matrix*, *Variety*, 29 March

MacDonald, M. (2000) 'Stimulation or Simulation? How to Deal with the Historical in the New Millennium', *Screen* Vol. 41, No. 1 (spring), pp. 108–15

McMahan, A. (2003) 'Immersion, Engagement, and Presence: A Method for Analyzing 3-D Video Games' in M.J.P. Wolf and B. Perron, eds, *The Video Game Theory Reader*, pp. 67–86. New York and London: Routledge

McPherson, T. (2002) 'Self, Other and Electronic Media' in D. Harries, ed., *The New Media Book*, pp. 183–94. London: BFI

Mak, M. (2003) 'Keeping Watch of Time: The Temporal Impact of the Digital in Cinema', *Convergence* Vol. 9, No. 4 (winter), pp. 38–47

Maltby, R. (1995) *Hollywood Cinema: An Introduction*. London: Arnold

Manovich, L. (2001) *The Language of New Media*. Cambridge, MA, and London: MIT

Manovich, Lev (2002), 'Old Media as New Media: Cinema' in D. Harries, ed., *The New Media Book*, pp. 209–18. London: BFI

Manovich, L. (2003) 'The Poetics of Augmented Space' in A. Everett and J.T. Caldwell, eds, *New Media: Theories and Practices of Digitextuality*, pp. 75–92. New York and London: Routledge

Marie, M. (2002) *The French New Wave: An Artistic School*. Oxford: Blackwell

Marshall, P.D. (2002) 'The New Intertextual Commodity' in D. Harries, ed., *The New Media Book*, pp. 69–81. London: BFI

Mayne, J. (1993) *Cinema and Spectatorship*. London and New York: Routledge

Meehan, E.R. (1991) '"Holy Commodity Fetish, Batman!": The Political Economy of a Commercial Intertext' in R.E. Pearson and W. Ulricchio, eds, *The Many Lives of the Batman*, pp. 47–65. London and New York: BFI and Routledge

Metz, C. (1974) 'Story and Discourse: Notes on Two Kinds of Voyeurism' in B. Nicholls, ed., *Movies and Methods: An Anthology Vol. 1*. London: University of California Press 1985

Miller, V. (2004) 'Stitching the Web into Global Capitalism: Two Stories' in D. Gauntlett and R. Harley, eds, *Web.Studies* 2nd edn., pp. 171–84. London: Arnold

Mitchell, W. J. (1992) *The Reconfigured Eye: Visual Truth in the Post-Photographic Era*. Cambridge, MA, and London: MIT Press

Monaco, J. (2000) *How to Read a Film: Movies, Media, Multimedia* 3rd edn. New York and Oxford: Oxford University Press

Morris, S. (2002) 'First-Person Shooters – A Game Apparatus' in G. King and T. Krzywinska, eds, *ScreenPlay: Cinema/Videogames/Interfaces*, pp. 81–97. London and New York: Wallflower

Morris, S. (2004) 'Co-Creative Media: Online Multiplayer Computer Game Culture', *Journal of Media Arts Culture*, Vol. 1, No. 1 (January), available online at: <http://www.scan.net.au/scan/journal/display_article.php?recordID=16>

MPAA (2006a) '2005 Theatrical Market Statistics', available online at: Motion Picture Association of America <http://www.mpaa.org/researchStatistics.asp>

MPAA (2006b) '2005 Movie Attendance Study', available online at: Motion Picture Association of America <http://www.mpaa.org/researchStatistics.asp>

Murch, W. (2001) *In the Blink of an Eye: A Perspective on Film Editing* 2nd edn. Los Angeles: Silman-James Press

Murray, J.H. (1997) *Hamlet on the Holodeck: The Future of Narrative in Cyberspace*. Cambridge, MA: MIT

Murray, S. (2003) 'Media Convergence's Third Wave: Content Streaming', *Convergence* Vol. 9, No. 1 (spring), pp. 8–18

Ndalianis, A. (2000) 'Special Effects, Morphing Magic, and the 1990s Cinema of Attractions' in V. Sobchack, ed., *Meta Morphing: Visual Transformation and the Culture of Quick-Change*. Minneapolis: University of Minneapolis Press

Neale, S. (1998) 'Widescreen Composition in the Age of Television' in S. Neale and M. Smith, eds, *Contemporary Hollywood Cinema*, pp. 130–41. London and New York: Routledge

Neale, S. and Smith, M. (1998), eds, *Contemporary Hollywood Cinema*. London and New York: Routledge

Negroponte, N. (1995) *Being Digital*. London: Coronet

Neupert, R. (2003) *A History of the French New Wave*. Madison: University of Wisconsin Press

Newman, J. (2004) *Videogames*. London and New York: Routledge

Newman, K. (1999) 'Time Machines', *Sight and Sound* Vol. 9, No. 4 (April), p. 11

North, D. (2005) 'Virtual Actors, Spectacle and Special Effects: Kung Fu Meets 'All that CGI Bullshit'' in S. Gillis, ed., *The Matrix Trilogy: Cyberpunk Reloaded*, pp. 48–61. London and New York: Wallflower

Nowell-Smith, G. and Thomas, P. (2003), eds, Special Issue, 'Digital Cinema', *Convergence* Vol. 9, No. 4 (winter)

Olsen, K.K. (2004) 'Copyright in Cyberspace: Protecting Intellectual Property Online' in D. Gauntlett and R. Harley, eds, *Web.Studies* 2nd edn., pp. 195–203. London: Arnold

Ondaatje, M (2002), ed., *The Conversations: Walter Murch and the Art of Film Editing*. London: Bloomsbury

Perron, B. (2003) 'From Gamers to Players and Gameplayers: The Example of Interactive Movies' in M.J.P. Wolf and B. Perron, eds, *The Video Game Theory Reader*, pp. 237–58. New York and London: Routledge

Persson, P. (2001) 'Cinema and Computers: Spatial Practices within Emergent Visual Technologies' in S.R. Munt, ed., *Technospaces*, pp. 38–56. London and New York: Continuum

Peters, M. (2003) 'Exit Meat: Digital Bodies in a Virtual World' in A. Everett and J.T. Caldwell, eds, *New Media: Theories and Practices of Digitextuality*, pp. 47–59. New York and London: Routledge

Pierson, M. (1999) 'CGI Effects in Hollywood Science-Fiction Cinema 1989–95: The Wonder Years', *Screen* Vol. 40, No. 2 (summer), pp. 158–76

Pierson, M. (2002) *Special Effects: Still in Search of Wonder*. New York: Columbia University Press

Poole, S. (2000) *Trigger Happy: The Inner Life of Videogames*. London: Fourth Estate

Pullen, K. (2000) 'I-love-Xena.com: Creating Online Fan Communities' in D. Gauntlett, ed., *Web.Studies: Rewiring Media Studies for the Digital Age*, pp. 52–61. London: Arnold

Pullen, K. (2004) 'Everybody's Gotta Love Somebody, Sometime: Online Fan Community' in D. Gauntlett and R. Harley, eds, *Web.Studies* 2nd edn., pp. 80–91. London: Arnold

Purse, L. (2005) 'The New Spatial Dynamics of the Bullet-Time Effect' in G. King, ed., *The Spectacle of the Real: From Hollywood to Reality TV and Beyond*, pp. 151–60. Bristol and Portland: Intellect

Rheingold, H. (1993) *Virtual Community: Homesteading on the Electronic Frontier*. Reading, MA: Addison Wesley

Richards, O. (2002) 'DVD Bonanza', *Empire* Issue 162 (December), pp. 146–7

Roberts, G. (2004) 'Movie-Making in the New Media Age' in D. Gauntlett and R. Harley, eds, *Web.Studies* 2nd edn., pp. 103–13. London: Arnold

Romney, J. (2003) 'Everywhere and Nowhere', *Sight and Sound* Vol. 13, No. 7 (July), pp. 24–7

Rosen, P. (2001) *Change Mummified: Cinema, Historicity, Theory*. Minneapolis and London: University of Minnesota Press

RSU (2005) Statistical Yearbook 2004/5, available online at: <http://www.filmcouncil.org.uk/statistics/yearbook>

Ryan, M.-L. (2001) *Narrative as Virtual Reality: Immersion and Interactivity in Literature and Electronic Media*. Baltimore and London: Johns Hopkins University Press

Sarafian, K. (2003) 'Flashing Digital Animations: Pixar's Digital Aesthetic' in A. Everett and J. T. Caldwell, eds, *New Media: Theories and Practices of Digitextuality*, pp. 209–23. New York and London: Routledge

Schatz, T. (1993) 'The New Hollywood' in J. Collins, H. Radner and A.P. Collins, eds, *Film Theory Goes to the Movies*, pp. 8–36. New York and London: Routledge

Schepelern, P. (2000) 'Film According to Dogma: Restrictions, Obstructions and Liberations', available online at: <http://www.dogme95.dk/news/interview/schepelern.htm>

Schleicher, S. (2001) 'Virtual Actors', available online at: <http://www.animationartist.com/2001/07_jul/features/Virtual/virtual_actors.htm>

Schwarzacher, L. (2004) 'Game Creator Ready for Pix', *Variety*, 28 Nov., available online at: <http://www.variety.com/article/VR1117914031?categoryid=1079&cs=1>

Seay, C. and Garrett, G. (2003) *The Gospel Reloaded: Exploring Spirituality and Faith in the Matrix*. Colorado Springs: Pinion

Sergi, G. (1998) 'A Cry in the Dark: The Role of Post-Classical Film Sound' in S. Neale and M. Smith, eds, *Contemporary Hollywood Cinema*, pp. 156–65. London and New York: Routledge

Sergi, G. (2001) 'The Sonic Playground: Hollywood Cinema and its Listeners' in M. Stokes and R. Maltby, eds, *Hollywood Spectatorship: Changing Perceptions of Cinema Audiences*, pp. 121–31. London: BFI

Sergi, G. (2004) *The Dolby Era: Film Sound in Contemporary Hollywood*. Manchester: Manchester University Press

Sheff, D. (1993) *Game Over: Nintendo's Battle to Dominate Videogames*. London: Hodder and Stoughton

Sheff, D. and Eddy, A. (1999) *Game Over: Press Start to Continue*. London: Cyberactive Media Group

Silberman, S. (2003) 'Matrix^2', available online at: <http://www.wired.com/wired/archive/11.05/matrix2_pr.html>

Silver, D. (2004) 'Internet/cyberculture/digital culture/new media/fill-in-the-blank studies', *New Media and Society* Vol. 6, No. 1 (February), pp. 55–64

Silverman, J. (2004) 'Brit Film Future is Digital', *Wired News* 18 Dec., available online at: <http://www.wired.com/news/digiwood/0,1412,66039.00.html>

Silverstone, R. (1999) 'What's New about New Media?', *New Media and Society* Vol. 1, No. 1 (April), pp. 10–12

Smith, A. (2004) 'R.I.P. VHS – Death of Video', *Empire* Issue 178 (April), pp. 107–15

Smith, J.H. (2002) 'Computer Game Research 101', available online at: <http//www.game-research.com/art_computer_game_research.asp>

Sobchack, V. (1993) *Screening Space: The American Science Fiction Film* 2nd edn. New York: Ungar

Speer, J. and O'Neill, C. (2000) 'The History of Resident Evil', available online at: <http://www.gamespot.com/gamespot/features/video/res-evil>

Spielman, Y. (2003) 'Elastic Cinema: Technological Imagery in Contemporary Science Fiction Films', *Convergence* Vol. 9, No. 3 (autumn), pp. 56–73

Stallabrass, J. (1996) *Gargantua: Manufactured Mass Culture*. London and New York: Verso

Stam, R. and Shohat, E.H. (2000) 'Film Theory and Spectatorship in the Age of the "Posts"' in C. Gledhill and L. Williams, eds, *Reinventing Film Studies*, pp. 381–401. London: Arnold

Stokes, M. and Maltby, R. (2001), eds, *Hollywood Spectatorship: Changing Perceptions of Cinema Audiences*. London: BFI

Telotte, J.P. (2001) '*The Blair Witch Project*: Film and the Internet', *Film Quarterly* Vol. 54, No. 3 (spring), pp. 32–9

Thompson, D. (2002) 'The Spider Stratagem', *Sight and Sound* Vol. 12, No. 4 (April), pp. 24–6

Thomson, D. (2001) 'Zap Happy: World War II Revisited', *Sight and Sound* Vol. 11, No. 7 (July), pp. 34–7

Thorburn, D. and Jenkins, H. (2003), eds, *Rethinking Media Change: The Aesthetics of Transition*. Cambridge, MA, and London: MIT

Tulloch, J. and Jenkins, H. (1995) *Science Fiction Audiences: Watching Doctor Who and Star Trek*. London and New York: Routledge

Turkle, S. (1997) *Life on the Screen: Identity in the Age of the Internet*. London: Phoenix

Turner, G. (2002) *The Film Cultures Reader*. London and New York: Routledge

UK Film Council (2005) '£12 Million Cinema-Going Revolution Begins in UK', available online at: <http://www.ukfilmcouncil.org.uk/funding/distributionandexhibition/dsn/>

Usai, P.C. (2001) *The Death of Cinema: History, Cultural Memory and the Digital Dark Age*. London: BFI

Verevis, C. (2005) 'Mike Figgis: *Timecode* and the Screen' in N. Rombes, ed., *New Punk Cinema*. Edinburgh: Edinburgh University Press

von Trier, L. and Vinterberg, T. (1995a) 'Index to The Vow of Chastity', available online at: <http://www.dogme95.dk/the_vow/index.htm>

von Trier, L. and Vinterberg, T. (1995b) 'The Vow of Chastity', available online at: <http://www.dogme95.dk/the_vow/vow.html>

Wasko, J. (1994) *Hollywood in the Information Age: Beyond the Silver Screen*. Cambridge: Polity

Wasko, J. (2002) 'The Future of Film Distribution and Exhibition' in D. Harries, ed., *The New Media Book*, pp. 195–206. London: BFI

Wells, P. (2001) *Animation: Genre and Authorship*. London: Wallflower

Willemen, P. (2004) 'Inflating the Narrator: Digital Hype and Allegorical Indexicality', *Convergence* Vol. 10, No. 3 (autumn), pp. 8–26

Willis, H. (2005) *New Digital Cinema: Reinventing the Moving Image.* London and New York: Wallflower

Winston, B. (1996) *Technologies of Seeing: Photography, Cinematography and Television.* London: BFI

Wolf, M.J.P. (2001a), ed., *The Medium of the Video Game.* Austin: University of Texas Press

Wolf, M.J.P. (2001b) 'The Video Game as a Medium' in M.J.P. Wolf, ed., *The Medium of the Video Game*, pp. 3–33. Austin: University of Texas Press

Wolf, M.J.P. (2001c) 'Space in the Video Game' in M.J.P. Wolf, ed., *The Medium of the Video Game*, pp. 51–75. Austin: University of Texas Press

Wolf, M.J.P. (2001d) 'Time in the Video Game' in M.J.P. Wolf, ed., *The Medium of the Video Game*, pp. 77–91. Austin: University of Texas Press

Wolf, M.J.P (2003a) 'Abstraction in the Video Game' in M.J.P. Wolf and B. Perron, eds, *The Video Game Theory Reader*, pp. 47–65. New York and London: Routledge

Wolf, M.J.P. (2003b) 'The Technological Construction of Performance', *Convergence* Vol. 9, No. 4 (winter), pp. 48–59

Wolf, M.J.P. and Perron, B. (2003a), eds, *The Video Game Theory Reader.* New York and London: Routledge

Wolf, M.J.P. and Perron, B. (2003b), 'Introduction' in M.J.P Wolf and B. Perron, eds, *The Video Game Theory Reader*, pp. 1–24. New York and London: Routledge

Wollen, P. (1980) 'Cinema and Technology: A Historical Overview' in T. de Lauretis and S. Heath, eds, *The Cinematic Apparatus*, pp. 14–25. London and Basingstoke: Macmillan

Wollen, T. (1993) 'The Bigger the Better: From CinemaScope to IMAX' in P. Hayward and T. Wollen, eds, *Future Visions: New Technologies of the Screen*, pp. 10–30. London: BFI

Wood, A. (2004) 'The Collapse of Reality and Illusion in *The Matrix*' in Y. Tasker, ed., *Action and Adventure Cinema*, pp. 119–29. London and New York: Routledge

Wood, A (2005) 'Vectorial Dynamics: Transtextuality and Complexity in the Matrix' in S. Gillis, ed., *The Matrix Trilogy: Cyberpunk Reloaded*, pp. 11–22. London and New York: Wallflower

Yeffeth, G. (2003), ed., *Taking the Red Pill: Science, Philosophy, and Religion in The Matrix.* Dallas: Benbella